Why You Should Read This Book as if Your Future in Selling Depended On It—What Salespeople Throughout the U.S. and Worldwide Say About It

"I've had your *No B.S. Sales Success* book in my possession for only three days. I have set up eight presentations, closed two deals. . . . the first presentation done the-Kennedy-way went off without a hitch because they were pre-sold before I arrived. That sale put **$13,475.00 profit in my pocket.**"

—Tom Halloran, Medical Supply Sales Rep, Phoenix, Arizona

"I have lived and worked in Australia, slugged it out on the street selling, to make a living. I knew there had to be an easier way, and I looked and looked for 25 years. When I found Dan Kennedy and adapted his unique way, my business took off like a cat on a hot tin roof in the outback. This year alone, Dan Kennedy was responsible for **adding more than one million dollars to my income—** and I never spoke to him!"

—Ed Burton, Financial/Investment/Asset Protection Advisor, Sydney, Australia

"My current success is entirely YOUR fault. I thank you so much. Changed my life. I'm not exaggerating. Your *No B.S. Sales Success* book is the #1 reason behind my success. I was born a big baby, 11.5 pounds, to a petite woman, my legs and feet grew crookedly inside her womb, and I had to wear special braces from birth to age 3 to straighten them out. My perfectionist father viewed me as a failure, according to the family, began drinking heavily after my birth, so I grew up with an alcoholic father. I feared rejection immensely, and practically lived inside my bedroom, hidden away from my father and the rest of the world as much as possible. I actually forced myself into sales to try and conquer my fears but I failed miserably, even declaring bankruptcy at age 21. I tried selling everything: cars, vacuum cleaners, insurance, you name it. One day I came across your book. One simple upgrade made in it changed my whole ʒʒʒʒ ʒting.'*

With guidance from your book, I specialized in a niche, I became an expert, I used my writing skills to create lead generation ads and free reports,** and began attracting pre-qualified prospects to me so I no longer had to prospect or ever feel rejected. I subsequently became THE top selling representative at a Fortune 500 company. Today, I've become a highly paid copywriter, selling via ads and sales letters. I have now specialized in marketing for cosmetic surgeons, and I am earning a fabulous income. Thank you, Dan, for everything."

—Michel Fortin, Ottawa, Ontario, Canada, www.SuccessDoctor.com
*Chapter #16. ** Chapter #17.

"One of your ideas got me one of the **biggest orders ever**—a whopping (for me) $17,001.00 check delivered by FedEx the first week I used your strategy!"

—Dick Miller, Wisconsin

"I'm a manufacturer's rep in the home furnishings industry. Your approach has **completely replaced cold prospecting**. In the past year, I've opened 22 new accounts, generated over $150,000.00 in new business, at a total cost of about $700.00 using your method."

—David Love, Davis, California

"I saw your Takeaway Selling advice to the lady dog trainer.*** You told her to give the dogs an IQ test before accepting them. Now my prospects must pass a test before they can buy from me! Thanks to this and other Kennedy strategies, my sales have multiplied, my little hobby is now a monster business, and it's all your fault."

—Glenn Osborn, Baltimore, MD, www.WeirdNLP.com
***Chapter #21

"Dan, just two words I gleaned from you **added almost $100,000.00** in income last year. My wife is thrilled. I bought her a new car."

—Chris Payne, LifeTools, Cheshire, U.K.

N●B.S. SALES SUCCESS

THE ULTIMATE
NO HOLDS BARRED
KICK BUTT
TAKE NO PRISONERS
& MAKE TONS
OF MONEY
GUIDE

Dan Kennedy

Entrepreneur.
Press

Editorial Director: Jere L. Calmes
Cover Design: David Shaw
Production and Composition: Eliot House Productions

This publication is designed to provide accurate and authoritative information in regard to the subject matter covered. It is sold with the understanding that the publisher is not engaged in rendering legal, accounting or
other professional services. If legal advice or other expert assistance is
required, the services of a competent professional person should be sought.

Library of Congress Cataloging-in-Publication Data
Kennedy, Dan S., 1954–
    No B.S. sales success: the ultimate no holds barred kick butt, take no
prisoners, and make tons of money guide/by Dan Kennedy
        p.   cm.
    ISBN 1-932156-89-5
    1. Selling. 2. Success in business. I. Title: Ultimate no holds barred
kick butt, take no prisoners, and make tons of money guide. II. Title.
HF5438.25.K473 2004
658.85—dc22   2004045554

Printed in Canada

09 08 07 06 05 04   10 9 8 7 6 5 4 3

Contents

PART 2

How to Stop Prospecting
Once and For All

PART 3

A No B.S. Start-to-Finish Structure for the Sale

Foreword
by Tom Hopkins

E very person who has chosen selling as a career must focus on getting the brass ring with every new contact they make. The brass ring for a salesperson is the closed sale. It's hearing the words, "yes," "we'll take it," or "how soon can it be delivered/installed/set up?" Those words, and a check, credit card, or purchase order to go with them, validate the salesperson. They demonstrate in both physical actions and words that the salesperson is representing something of value to the client— so much value that the client is willing to exchange their security (spelled M-O-N-E-Y) for it. It also demonstrates that the salesperson did a good job, using their skills and talents in presenting the product in such a way that the client saw how the benefits it would provide fulfilled a need. Having a client say, "thank you" tells you they're happy the salesperson brought it their way. That "thank you" is like getting a standing ovation.

There's a lot of psychology behind what works and doesn't work in selling. It has to do with mindsets (both yours and the client's), attitude, fears, perception, body language, voice, vocabulary, style, grooming, expectations, preparation, and too many other aspects to list here. An entire encyclopedia of selling could be written if every little nuance of selling was to be taught. It might take you a few years to read such a series of books.

My questions to you is, do you want to take the course in psychology to understand what's behind the sales process or do you just want to hear what works? If you're like most salespeople, you're looking for the shortest route between where you are now and increased sales. That's the benefit of this book. Dan has literally eliminated the B.S. in explaining great ways to make more sales.

We can learn many things simply by reading, but we only benefit if we invest time in thinking about what we've read and how it applies to what we're doing. We excel when we put the knowledge gained to use. This is a relatively short book. Invest your time wisely in reading it with thoughtfulness about how you can apply the strategies it contains. You'll be glad you did.

Tom Hopkins is world-renowned as a master sales trainer. *Sell It Today, Sell It Now,* on compact disc and co-authored by Pat Leiby, is an excellent resource for learning how to lower sales resistance and increase sales acceptance in potential clients. For more information, contact him at info@tomhopkins.com. Receive free sales content, tips, and closes by subscribing to Tom's selling skills e-newsletter at http://www.tomhopkins.com.

Preface

There are basically four types of salespeople: sales professionals with strong ambition who are eager to strengthen and fine-tune their skills; sales professionals who are jaded, close-minded, cynical, and stuck; nonsalespeople who realize they need to be, such as doctors, auto repair shop owners, carpet cleaners; and nonsalespeople who either do not recognize they need to be or are resistant to the idea.

Ambitious Salespeople 1	2 Stuck Salespeople
3 Nonsalespeople Eager to Learn	4 Resistant Nonsalespeople

This book will resonate with those in the first and third quadrant. It will be wasted on the others. I've spent more than one-fourth of an entire lifetime, more than 25 years, working with people in both the first and third quadrant—and doing my level best to avoid the folks in the second and fourth. This book literally summarizes the most important strategies I've developed over those 25 years—some originating from my own experience, others originating from my observation of super-successful sales pros' behaviors that I have converted to replicatable strategy.

There are a great many things this book is NOT. It is NOT, for example, a textbook approach to selling. It is not about moral or spiritual philosophy (those matters are left to you). It is only slightly about the psychology of selling. It is noticeably free of trendy new terminology, buzzwords, and psycho-babble so many sales trainers and authors seem to be fond of. And it is not a motivational book either. If you need someone else to motivate you, you have far bigger problems than this book might tackle. Or any hundred books, for that matter.

This is simply a straightforward, relentlessly pragmatic, "no b.s." presentation of what REALLY works in selling. Not what should work. Not the academic theories about selling. What REALLY works.

You may not thoroughly enjoy this book. It may make you uncomfortable. Confronting, challenging, and rethinking long-held beliefs and habits is provocative and often profitable but rarely comfortable or enjoyable.

My aim is very simple: after reading this book, I intend for you to implement behavioral and procedural changes that will immediately and dramatically increase the income you earn from selling. This book is all about putting more money in your pocket, nothing loftier than that, nothing less than that. And if we have to break a few eggs to make that omelet, then that's what we'll do.

You might want to know that this book has had a long former life. It was first published in 1994, has been in print continuously through 1996, a 2nd edition was published in 1999, which was in print through 2001, and now this thoroughly updated and sub-stantially expanded in this new edition. Why is it important for you to know you've wound up with "the sales book that will not die" in your hands? Two reasons. First, as evidence you've got-ten your paws on strategies that ARE really valuable and that DO really work. Successful salespeople recommend this book to each other, they stream to the bookstores and demand it. Even when a publisher has lost interest in it, the marketplace has insisted this book be put back onto the store shelves. (By the way, now you can tell others about this book by sending them to www.nobsbooks. com, to get free excerpts.) Second, you will see references in the book that are obviously dated, or references to my writing of its first edition, and I didn't want you to be confused by that; thus, this explanation.

Now, to the important stuff: quick, practical actions you can take to make selling easier, less stressful, more fun, and much, much more lucrative and rewarding.

About the Structure of This Book

This book is divided into six parts. In Part 1, I describe the 15 strategies I use most in selling. Each is a stand-alone application, and any one of them alone could significantly improve your results in selling. But they can also be linked together differently for different situations for increased value and power.

In Part 2, I deal with what goes on before selling can even begin: finding, attracting, and getting into a selling situation with a prospect. As you'll see, I'm no fan of the way most salespeople carry out this job. Here you'll discover some rather radical ideas.

In Part 3, I provide a framework for selling. The various pieces described in Parts 1 and 2 can be plugged in and out of this structure.

In Part 4, I share with you the dumbest things salespeople do to sabotage themselves.

In Part 5, I reveal my personal, best, most valued, contrary approach to selling. It may not be for everybody; it may not be for you. Frankly, I argued with myself about putting it in or leaving it out. I ultimately decided I would not be playing fair with you if I sold you a book about selling and held back the information most responsible for my own success. Use it as you will, and good luck.

In the last decade, the sales world has been flooded with new technology, and Part 6 of this edition contains an updated section on my "no b.s." observations of this.

—Dan S. Kennedy

PART 1

15 No B.S. Strategies
for Exceptional Success
in Sales, Persuasion,
and Negotiations

CHAPTER 1

Strategy 1
Ignoring the Word "No"

My first sales position (and the only time I've been employed by someone else) was a wonderful training ground. I learned a lot from my experiences in that position, and you'll notice throughout this book that I refer to it several times.

I was hired as the central states sales representative for a Los Angeles-based book publisher. I was assigned Ohio, Kentucky, Indiana, Michigan, and Pennsylvania. My job was to call on all the bookstores, department store book departments, discount stores, gift shops, and other retailers in that territory to service existing accounts and open new ones. Most of the company's books were humorous, impulse-purchase items. In many stores, the line of books was merchandised on the publisher's six-foot-high spinner racks, which I had to inventory and stock.

One minor fact that was not discussed when I was hired was that my territory had been "orphaned," and the established accounts had received no service of any kind for eight months or longer. I soon discovered that some of the accounts were a trifle annoyed at having been sold this line of merchandise, promised service, and then ignored.

I was furnished with a computer printout of all the accounts and their purchase history. The first one I visited, a drugstore, provided a clue that things might not be well. I walked up to the owner, introduced myself as the new representative from the company, and watched a mild-mannered pharmacist turn into a raving lunatic. He grabbed me by the arm and dragged me into the back room where he showed me a pile of rack parts that had been shipped in, but that he had been unable to assemble. Surrounding that mess was a stack of boxes full of books. He told me that he had been invoiced for books and racks and had been dunned by a collector for payment, even though he had never had a chance to get the books on the floor to sell. He literally threw the rack parts out of the back door while screaming at me to take it all away.

In the next few weeks, I met with similar antagonism at almost every account I called on. I took a lot of racks and a lot of inventory out of stores. Besides being generally unpleasant and occasionally hazardous to my health, this situation was an economic disaster. I was being rated as a sales rep, and my bonuses were based on a "positive sales ratio" for the month. That means: sales less returns equal net sales.

The way I was going, I would have a negative sales figure for my first month—maybe my first year. I determined that something had to change, and I had to be the one to create the change.

That decision alone is an important tip about getting your own way. It doesn't much matter whether we're talking about selling like the work I was doing, or negotiating business deals, or running a business. Anybody can look good and get good results when everybody else is cooperating and everything is going as it is supposed to. Under those conditions, just about anybody can have a good time and make a lot of money.

This often happens in business. When times are good, the CEO looks like a genius, and the sales reps look like superstars. But when the first rough waters come along, these same people suddenly look like bumbling idiots. Have they actually changed that much? No—they were never very sharp in the first place.

I made up my mind that I had to sell these angry, neglected customers on keeping our line in their stores and even buying more. I had to get positive results under these very negative circumstances. I had to face customers who had been lied to, inconvenienced,

---

Dan Kennedy's #1 No B.S. Truth About Selling

If you're going to achieve high levels of success in selling, you've got to be able to get positive results under negative circumstances.

---

billed for merchandise they couldn't sell, dunned for payment, and otherwise abused, and somehow get them to "forgive and forget." In order to do this, *I had to take my ego out of the way.*

Since I've been involved in training salespeople and working with sales executives struggling to get productivity from salespeople, I've discovered that the number one reason for failure in selling is ego. The person with an inflated ego or with very fragile self-esteem (the two are connected) *perceives refusal as rejection.* When someone says no to such a person, he or she takes it personally.

But confusing refusal with rejection makes selling painful because more people say no than ever say yes. In my situation, customers were calling me vile names, threatening me, even throwing things at me. I had to remember that it really had nothing to do with me. These people weren't mad at me; they were mad at the previous rep, at the company, or at the situation—but not at me.

I've since learned that just about any time an individual disagrees with me, fails to accept an offer I present, says no to me, or otherwise interferes with my access to what I want, it very rarely has anything to do with me as a person. And because it isn't personal, it doesn't warrant any kind of an emotional reaction. Having control over your emotions gives you a very powerful advantage in selling.

As I approached these hostile customers, I took my emotions out of the situation. No matter what they said, I interpreted it as reasonable, justifiable anger at other people and at a negative situation. I listened. I was patient. I was concerned. And I never got angry. I never got defensive. Finally, when the customer had vented and had nothing more to say, I asked for permission to respond. I stated the obvious: I had no control over the past. I could only exercise control over the present. My job now was to make handling the merchandise so profitable and pleasurable for the merchant that it made up for all the past problems and justified a renewed relationship. Then I shifted right into selling—just as if the customer was new and had never heard of the company, the books, or me.

It worked. But even while it was working, many of the customers questioned my integrity. They wanted to know whether or not I was telling the truth. They asked whether I would keep my promises concerning service. They were skeptical and suspicious. If I had wanted to be thin-skinned, I could have gotten angry with them. How dare they question *my* honesty?

Again, I had to understand that this, too, was nothing personal. I chose to work for a company that had "done them wrong" once. I had to accept the consequences, including guilt by association. Again, I had to set my ego aside.

With this approach, I saved twice as many accounts as I lost. I even returned to that first drugstore and got the merchandise back in. I had discovered that initial refusal, even antagonism, was not necessarily the ultimate result. I discovered that I could change a no to a yes more often than not.

My favorite illustration of all this comes from my first call on the head buyer for the book departments of a major department store chain. I went with one of the company's experienced salespeople, as an apprentice, to watch and learn. I was to carry the samples and keep my mouth shut.

Keeping quiet was no problem; I sat in stunned silence as the other sales rep presented the buyer with one new title after another. As he looked at each book, the buyer kept saying: "This is crap. Do you know that? Why should I have this crap in my store? How can you show me this crap?" The buyer went on and on like that, and the sales rep did not say a word! Finally, the buyer picked up one sample after the other and barked: "Ship me ten dozen" or "ship me 50." This went on for nearly an hour, and the sales rep rarely spoke. The buyer criticized and cussed each sample, then ordered. When it was over, the rep had written an order for close to $10,000.00—a very, very big order in that business. He and the buyer shook hands, exchanged pleasantries, and we left. I couldn't believe what I had witnessed.

The sales rep said, "You know, he always does that. The first few times I went in there, years ago, I got mad at him. I got defensive. I argued with him. Finally he took pity on me. He asked me a great question: "What do you care what I think of this stuff or say about this stuff as long as I buy a lot of it and my stores sell a lot of it and you make a lot of money?"

I have been a very serious student of Dr. Maxwell Maltz's work since I was in my teens. Dr. Maltz's best known book, *Psycho-Cybernetics*, has sold more than 30 million copies worldwide. His works have had such important impact on me that several years ago I acquired all the rights to all his works, now control their distribution, and have co-authored new ones (check out www.psycho-cybernetics.com for more information). One of the key things I learned from *Psycho-Cybernetics* was how to develop a strong self-image bullet-proof against all unimportant criticism. I have also long been a very serious student of first-generation millionaires who've gotten there by building businesses from scratch. I now have had more than 100 such people as clients and associates, and developed my *Renegade Millionaire System* based on them. (You can learn more about my system at www.renegade millionaire.com.) A common trait found in the majority of these people is a strong immunity to criticism. This is a theme you'll find running through the top performers in selling as well. They care little about what people *think*; they care about what people *buy*.

Nos Turned Into Yeses,
That's What Master Salespeople Do

For ten years, recently concluded at my choice, I had the great privilege of touring North America, appearing as a speaker on seminar programs with legendary sales and success speaker Zig Ziglar, as well as Brian Tracy, Jim Rohn, Tom Hopkins, and numerous celebrities, addressing audiences of as many as 35,000 people in each city. Zig is one of the "masters" I studied at the very beginning of my selling life. One of his stories that stuck in my mind permanently features the saleswoman who couldn't hear a no shouted in her ear but could hear a whispered yes from 50 paces. That is the right approach: Simply ignore the word no.

People start out by saying no to things for many, many reasons. It's sort of an automatic, knee-jerk, defense mechanism. They may not fully understand the matter you are dealing with and be too embarrassed to admit it. They may not know how to intelligently make a decision. They may lack self-confidence and self-esteem. They may be afraid. They may have financial problems that (in their minds) preclude them from going along with you. There are probably hundreds of possible reasons for "the erroneous no." Don't let it stop you.

Eight Steps for Getting Past No

1. Determine that you are going to exert control over the situation and the other people involved.
2. Determine that you can and will get positive results even in negative situations.
3. Get your ego out of the way.
4. Do not confuse refusal with rejection.
5. Be more interested in achieving positive results than in anything else.

6. Understand that most no's are erroneous.
7. Ignore the "erroneous no." Keep making your case. Keep probing for the real reason for reluctance or refusal.
8. Respond only to real reasons. Don't get caught up in responding to "erroneous no's"—that's like wrestling with a phantom.

Understanding, remembering, and using these eight steps will help you convert many refusals to ultimate acceptance. However, having said all this, a much, much smarter approach is to place yourself in Low-Resistance Selling Situations, where these techniques aren't required at all. A great deal of traditional sales training focuses on "closing," but I maintain if you need to close, you opened poorly. The close should be effortless, painless, automatic. As you'll discover, the vast majority of this book is devoted to helping you engineer Low-Resistance Selling Situations rather than succeeding in tough sales situations.

Still, having said that, every so often, you will find yourself up against the "tough customer." When that occurs, ignoring no is a giant step toward yes.

CHAPTER 2

Strategy 2
The Positive Power
of Negative Preparation

I 've been involved in what I've labeled "the success education business" since 1976. Since 1978, I've been an active member of the National Speakers Association—fraternizing and consulting with hundreds of people who earn their livings as professional lecturers and seminar leaders, including some whose names you know. During that time, I've spoken to nearly 6,000,000 people from the platform, maybe more, about success-oriented topics. I've delivered as many as 100 speaking presentations a year for major corporations and associations and at large public events; only in the past couple of years have I deliberately cut back that pace.

I have frequently been mislabeled and misintroduced as a "motivational speaker" from the platform, in meetings, at cocktail parties. As a result, I've had more conversations than I care to count with my students, clients, customers, peers, and friends about "positive thinking." Through it all, I've come to the conclusion that at least 95% of the people who think they're positive thinkers actually have no idea what positive thinking is really all about.

Too many people think it's some kind of mystical, magical shield from the real world. They believe that if they just think positive, bad things cannot happen to them. If something bad happens to somebody, they say: "See, you weren't thinking positively." But it just doesn't work that way. You can think positively until you are turning blue from the effort, but you'll still run into obstacles from time to time. People who believe that positive thinking is supposed to keep the bogeyman away eventually wind up frustrated, discouraged critics of positive thinking.

Being a positive thinker does not mean that you should refuse to acknowledge the way things are. In fact, people succeed in business, sales, and marketing by dealing with "what is" not with "what ought to be." The true positive thinker acknowledges potential and existing negative circumstances and reactions, and engineers a plan to overcome them to achieve positive results. In selling or negotiating, I call this the *positive power of negative preparation.*

How General Patton Used the
Positive Power of Negative Preparation

There's a great sequence in the movie Patton where General Patton is dozing the night before a battle. He has Field Marshal

Rommel's book on tactics in his lap. The next day, Patton's troops drive Rommel's troops off the battlefield into retreat. As the gunfire and other noise ends, Patton is standing alone, leaning forward, stage whispering across the battlefield:

"Rommel—I read your book."

Some people would say that acknowledging Rommel's expertise as a tactician and preparing to counter any possible successful moves was being negative. They're wrong. It was positively brilliant.

In several of the most successful, profitable, complex negotiations I've been involved in—buying and selling businesses; assembling capital; developing relationships with celebrities, manufacturers, and producers in the TV infomercial business—I've prepared by anticipating and writing down every possible question, concern, and objection the other party could raise, and then formulating my responses in advance. I carefully analyzed every weakness in my position that might be attacked and thought of ways to respond effectively. I thought of every possible thing that could screw up the deal and then thought of some preventive measure to take in each case. I was thoroughly prepared, from a negative perspective.

In 1999, I sold one of my companies—that entire process, from first approaching my chosen buyer to cashing the check, took only six days. In 2003, I sold another of my businesses, in less than 20 days. These are typically complex sales situations fraught with peril, from deal-killing lawyers to hidden agendas to misunderstandings, and on and on. The speed with which I completed these sales is testament in large part to careful negative preparation.

Who Else Uses the Positive Power of Negative Preparation?

I'm a bit of a sports freak, and as a speaker, I've had the terrific opportunity of spending time backstage in "the green room" with champion athletes like Troy Aikman, Joe Montana, George Foreman, Mary Lou Retton, and with top coaches including Lou Holtz, Jimmy Johnson, and the late Tom Landry. My friends in the world of sports have included Brendan Suhr, who has been an assistant head coach of three NBA teams; and Bill Foster, former head basketball coach at Northwestern University and one of the "winningest" coaches in college basketball.

I have talked about this subject with all of them and found consensus. These champions have super-strength positive attitudes, but they also wisely use the positive power of negative preparation.

Most successful coaches go into each game with more than one prepared game plan. They have a plan to follow if their team gets ahead early in the game. They have a different plan to follow if their team falls behind. They have alternate plans ready to use different combinations of players in case one key player is injured during the game. That's not negative thinking; that's the positive power of negative preparation at work.

I've done a lot of work in planning, scripting, and implementing group sales presentations and training others to do the same. What I call "group presentation marketing" applies to everything from a Tupperware party to a seminar designed to sell $50,000.00 real estate partnerships. There are a lot of special techniques for this type of marketing, but one of the most important is the anticipation and removal of the reasons for refusal or procrastination on the audience's part. Sometimes this is done with subtlety, weaving the objections and responses into the presentation. Other times it's done quite openly. One very successful presentation I designed ended with the presenter listing on the flip-chart the four main reasons why people don't join—and then answering every one of them. But in every case, every possible problem was thought out in advance and countered somehow during the presentation.

You also have to do this when you are selling in print. I am paid from a $15,000.00 to $70,000.00 plus royalties as a direct-response copywriter to write full-page newspaper and magazine ads, sales letters, infomercials, and other marketing documents. More than 85% of all clients who use me once do so repeatedly—in spite of my high fees. Why? One reason is my very thorough negative preparation. When I'm creating an advertisement, brochure, or direct-mail piece, I make a list of every reason I can think of why the reader would not respond to the offer. I use that list of "negatives" as a guide in writing the copy. And the other top direct-response copywriters I know, like my friend John Carlton, also carefully consider these potential obstacles to the sale when crafting a message. This approach produces some of the most powerful selling techniques in print in the world.

If this strategy is important to us, the people behind the scenes who get paid as much to write one sales letter as many professionals earn in six months, then it is important to you, too!

Six Steps for Using the Positive Power of Negative Preparation

1. Forget preconceived labels of "positive" or "negative."
2. Make a list of every question, concern, or objection that the other person could possibly come up with.

3. Make a list of everything that could go wrong.
4. Develop positive responses to all the negatives you've thought of.
5. Have your information, ideas, and documentation well organized so you can lay your hands on the appropriate notes and materials at a moment's notice.
6. Take great confidence from your thorough preparation.

CHAPTER 3

Strategy 3
Use Listening to
Influence People

H ere's my super-powerful secret selling weapon: I listen.

Listening isn't as simple as it sounds. In fact, the absence of good listening skills is rated as one of the top problems in North American business today. Some major corporations invest huge sums of money in listening skills training for their personnel. My biggest complaint with people I work with is their lack of listening effectiveness; I explain something deliberately and precisely, but they get only part of what I'm saying. So, the first problem is that most people lack know-how in listening.

The second problem is even those people who CAN listen often DON'T, for many reasons. Let's look at some of the most common reasons people don't listen.

They Are Preoccupied with Other Thoughts

If you could see what was going on in the other person's mind, like images on a TV screen, you'd be shocked. Something related to what you are saying might appear every once in a while, but there'd be a rush of other, unrelated images in between.

When I'm speaking to an audience, I know that a fast-paced parade of images is going through their heads: a kitchen on fire—"Gee, I wonder if I turned off the coffee pot?"; the supermarket—"What should I make for dinner?"; an angry spouse slamming the door—"She's so unreasonable"; and on and on. They leave me and my presentation mentally, then come back, leave again, and come back. In fact, psychologists say people mentally leave every four to eight minutes for sexual fantasy. The good news is, I know everybody in the audience will have a good time regardless of what I do. The bad news is, I'm up there to sell and need their attention.

The sales pro has to master methods for disconnecting all those other thoughts and focusing entirely and exclusively on the prospect or client.

They Are Tired

I'm guilty of this myself. After a few days of traveling, speaking, and consulting, a level of fatigue sets in that just about ruins my ability to listen.

It's worth noting that being properly rested and alert is an advantage in selling or negotiating. The sales pro who stays up too late night after night, schedules important meetings too close together, or employs an excessively exhausting travel schedule starts each selling situation with a handicap. Personally, I find both travel and selling activity require incredible physical energy. Avoiding fatigue-inducing foods, sticking to a healthy diet as best I can, seeing my chiropractor and massage therapist regularly, and taking carefully selected nutritional supplements are all lifestyle techniques I believe give me an edge in my selling activities.

They Are in Too Much of a Hurry

It is easy and dangerous to be consumed by speed rather than to profit from efficiency. These days, it seems the sales pro never gets a breather; he lets his cell phone, beeper, e-mail control him; he tries to run marathons as sprints. The trick is to use speed to your advantage and to prevent it from becoming a disadvantage. If you have a tendency, as I do, to get caught up in the pace of things going on around you and to build up stress in the process, it's important to consciously s-l-o-w y-o-u-r-s-e-l-f d-o-w-n in most selling situations. Listening effectively cannot be done at warp speed. You have to disengage from the race pace and shift into a relaxed selling pace. Another way of saying this is "letting the sale come to you."

They Are Unable to Focus Their Attention

Many adults today have very poor attention spans. TV advertisers are well aware of this, and the need to bring commercials up to "MTV speed" was a topic of hot discussion in the advertising business when I wrote the first edition of this book. True "talk shows" hosted by highly skilled interviewers like Dick Cavett or Charlie Rose can exist only on PBS. Video games and the habit of "clicking" through the TV dial with the remote condition people to low attention spans.

As a result of all this, nobody's listening to anybody. And because people generally want most what they have the least of, many are running around in desperate search of—anyone—who will make them feel important by listening to what they have to say. There is enormous opportunity in knowing and understanding that.

By training and disciplining myself to listen—really listen— I've been able to exert tremendous influence over many other people. I've gained their trust, stimulated friendship, gotten them to confide in me, and sold to them with ease. I've discovered that you can exchange attention for dollars! I'm now convinced that the person who gets his or her own way most often is the person doing a lot more listening than talking.

Incidentally, should you ever seek to seduce someone, this is the secret to doing so quickly and certainly. Nothing is more flattering and compelling to a person than having someone else clearly, totally, unwaveringly focused on, "into," intently listening to them. I have an interesting, controversial friend you may have seen on TV talk shows, Ross Jeffries, who teaches men what he calls "Speed Seduction." A key component of his "system" is paying highly focused attention to the other person.

What Are You Listening For?

In selling, you should be listening with purpose. Not just to build rapport, not to be polite, not to flatter, not to seduce, but more for strategic acquisition of important and useful information. I've labeled this "Listening-Based Selling," and taught it to thousands of salespeople. In doing so, I discovered a crying need for a "tool" to support Listening-Based Selling.

If you don't know what you hope to hear, you might not recognize it when you do hear it. I've compiled a checklist of 21 things to listen for, which you can download free at www.nobsbooks.com. For now, here are several of the most important things to listen for:

- What keeps him up at night unable to sleep, bile crawling up his esophagus from frustration, anger, and resentment? (Note: Relief of pain sells more than potential gain.)
- What does he fear and worry about most? (Note: Fear is the most powerful of all motivational forces.)
- What overriding value is most important to him, as demonstrated by his behavior and prioritized actions, not just lip service—is it family, marriage, career achievement, wealth, security, what?

There are 18 others. My 21 may or may not all apply to your particular selling situation, so, ultimately, you should construct and memorize your own checklist. Then you'll listen with purpose. And you'll be able to quantify and measure your listening effectiveness. After a first conversation with a client, I measure mine by how many of the 21 things I was listening for I heard and remembered. Because measurement automatically improves performance, you'll become a much more effective listener with this discipline.

How to Read Anyone's Mind

Early in my business life, I traveled to New York to a private meeting at the palatial office of the CEO of a large, fast-growing

Dan Kennedy's #2 No B.S. Truth About Selling

You don't have to be a psychic to read someone's mind—he or she will read it out loud to you, with a little encouragement!

public company. I was being considered for a very important, very big, very lucrative consulting assignment, potentially worth hundreds of thousands of dollars to me. In the 40 minutes or so of this meeting, we actually dealt with the matter at hand for only ten minutes, and I listened for half of those minutes. For the other half hour, I mostly listened to the CEO talk about his problems of the day, expound on his business philosophy, brag about his most recent big deal, and unintentionally tell me exactly what he wanted to hear from me to make our deal. I sat there and quietly "read his mind."

In 1993, I wrote a small book about this subject: *How to Read Anyone's Mind*. It has been out of print for years, but now you have it, as a "Bonus Book," at the end of this one. I have added a few updated references but largely preserved the original text as it was.

Five Steps to Listening More Effectively

1. Clear your mind of distractions before getting into a meeting with another person or other people. Take a minute to close your eyes and blank your mind immediately before

going into a meeting or picking up the telephone. Top tele-marketing trainers tell people handling incoming calls to set aside their paperwork on the first ring, close their eyes and take a deep breath on the second ring, then smile and answer on the third ring.

2. Determine in advance why the person you are going to be listening to is important to you and why what he or she is saying might be important to you. You have to sell yourself on the relevance in order to focus your attention.

3. Listen for information and insight that you can use to engineer cooperation with the other person. A long, apparently irrelevant, favorite story told by the other person may inadvertently reveal one tiny clue to effectively persuading or motivating that person.

4. Be an active listener. Nod. Give feedback. Ask questions to encourage the person to continue and to demonstrate your interest. Use the technique of "mirroring" to put the other person at ease. Mirroring is a Neuro-Linguistic Programming (NLP) term. Many sales professionals, speakers, and negotiators study and employ NLP techniques. This is not to advise sacrificing personality and individuality. I certainly haven't, and I don't believe anybody else should. But you can keep your individuality and still modify your physiology, within a range, to make the person you are listening to feel more comfortable.

5. In some business situations, it may be appropriate to jot down notes as you listen. Don't hesitate to do so; it helps illustrate your interest.

CHAPTER 4

Strategy 4
Avoid Contamination

I n just about every sales organization lurk "grizzled veterans" who, through a combination of longevity, seniority, and accumulated customers or clients, manage to earn reasonably good livings even though they are poor salespeople. These hangers-on make money in spite of their many bad habits. *These people are extremely dangerous to the fresh, enthusiastic salesperson* for a number of reasons.

- They are not fully aware of all their own counter-productive attitudes and habits, and they are capable of unintentionally contaminating others.

- They resent hotshots who might make them look lazy, ineffective, or over-the-hill, and will consciously and subconsciously do things to put the hotshot in his or her place.

- They do not keep up-to-date and informed on the latest sales techniques and product information, so they are likely to be sources of outdated or inaccurate information, even when they sound authoritative and knowledgeable.

- They often have very poor personal habits, including drinking at lunch and after work on a daily basis, using foul language, and sometimes even poor personal hygiene.

- They are cynical about people. They often call customers or clients "marks," "pigeons," and other derogatory names. *You cannot succeed in selling in a big way if you are cynical about people or about your clientele.* (Note that it's OK to be realistic, just not cynical; there is a difference.)

- They are complainers and blamers—that's how they excuse their own mediocrity. In order to succeed in selling, you must take full responsibility for every factor in the process.

Every business, every company, every organization has at least a few of these types. You will find them on the showroom floor at the car dealership, gathered around the coffee machine in the real estate office, in the hall, or at the sales meeting. You must not let these people contaminate you! You must not let them poison your well!

Very recently, I worked with a client stuck with three veteran salespeople stubbornly unwilling to make outbound telephone calls generated by the advertising I'd developed. They insisted these were poor quality leads, "mooches" as they put it, who had requested free books and tapes from the ads but had no real interest in the high-priced product being sold. At my urging, he hired three new, additional salespeople just to follow up on these leads—but he put them in the same office as the first two. In less than two weeks, the old vets ruined the new ones. The new reps had a brief, initial flurry of success, then their results diminished. Later, we again got three new salespeople and installed them in a distant building; they produced millions of dollars of business from those "mooches." Old dogs who refuse to learn new tricks should never be permitted to raise puppies.

How to Cheat on Your Expense Account and Other "Lessons" from the Grizzled Old Pro

Early in my selling career, a manager flew in to work with me in my territory. He and I traveled together for a week. He taught me several creative ways to cheat on my expense account and how to make sales calls by phone and write them up as if they were made in person. He taught me virtually nothing about selling. He was a great "pal." He had a terrific if slightly bizarre sense of humor, and he was making reasonably good money. But he had nothing to offer that would help me achieve my goals.

Shortly after being hired, I went to Chicago to work the company's exhibit booth in the Chicago Gift Show. This is a huge trade show, where tens of thousands of gift shop owners and chain store buyers come in search of new, different, and sellable merchandise. I was excited about being there and eager to write a lot of business with the people attending from my territory. Almost instantly, the other sales pros ganged up on me, saying things like, "Take it easy—we're gonna be here for four long days"; "Don't be too aggressive—it looks bad"; "Most of these people are just lookers, not buyers, anyway"; "Nobody sells much at these shows—we're here to get leads."

I ignored the whole bunch of them and, much to their irritation, wrote thousands of dollars of orders during the show. No huge amount—nothing to write home about—but it was more than what five of the others (who had at least six years more experience than I did) made.

Those experiences taught me that it was generally unwise to listen to advice, complaints, and comments of others just because they were older or more experienced. Age is not necessarily equivalent to wisdom. Experience does not always teach much. In fact, since most people stop learning very early in their careers, you are very likely to encounter a person who has one year's experience 30 times rather than 30 years of experience.

You must exercise great care in selecting those who are permitted to advise and influence you. Falling under the influence of someone headed nowhere will generally lead you to the same destination!

Dan Kennedy's #3
No B.S. Truth About Selling

It's a good idea to learn from other people's experience but usually with this caveat: seek out and learn from those with experience who are at the top of their game.

There is probably no profession other than selling where mental attitude is as important. The late W. Clement Stone was a self-made multimillionaire who began as a star insurance sales pro and taught tens of thousands of others how to excel in that field while building the largest independent insurance sales organization of its time out of the depths of the Great Depression. He summed it up this way: "The sale is contingent on the attitude of the salesperson, not the prospect." It is for that reason that you must militantly protect your mental attitude from contamination. Your success will be contingent on *your* mental attitude, not the attitude of your customers or clients.

Oh, and incidentally, Stone didn't say, "The sale is contingent upon the attitude of the salesperson, not the prospect—unless times are tough, unless there's recession, unless there's a tough competitor in the game, unless..." No weasel words, no escape clause here.

CHAPTER 5

Strategy 5
The Process of
Personal Packaging

I have a lot of experience in the advertising business, so I often
think in terms of advertising. One big factor in the advertising and marketing of most products is packaging. Different
packaging is appropriate for different products. Sometimes different packaging for the same product works better in different
geographic areas. There are many variables to consider. I think
these same considerations apply to packaging yourself.

Like everybody else, I have strong personal preferences
about clothing and fashion. I like certain things; I dislike other
things. I'm sure you do, too. However, *the successful sales pro
learns to set aside his preferences in favor of the most effective and*

appropriate personal packaging for a given situation. You might think of this as image management. It is critically important.

A prime consideration when packaging yourself is the first impression you give others. Psychologists tell us that most people form impressions of others in the first four minutes of meeting them and that 80% of the impression is based on nonverbal input. What you say has very little to do with it. We also know that people are very reluctant to change their first impressions.

Another consideration is the overall, continuing impression you communicate. You need to always be thinking about what your appearance says about you.

A Valuable Lesson from a Prejudiced Banker

Early in the operation of my first business—an ad agency—my Monday mail brought back a client's check for a sizable amount marked NSF. (That means "non-sufficient funds," although I'm told that in the South it means "not so fast!") This was not good news. So I jumped in my car and took my client's bad check to his bank, hoping there might be some money passing through that I could intercept. I sat down across the desk from the bank's vice president, passed him his customer's bad check, and told him my story.

The banker said, "As I'm sure you can appreciate, this is the type of matter we prefer to discuss only with the principals of the firms involved."

I handed him my business card and said, "I'm president of the agency. I'm the principal. Let's talk."

He said, in a sincerely surprised voice, "You can't be president; you're not wearing a tie."

Of course, I stomped and growled and slammed angrily out of the bank. But later, when I calmed down, I dealt with several interesting issues about success.

For Every One Person Who Says It, There Are Somewhere Between 10 and 10,000 Who Think It

All marketing research is based on that premise, and I believe it is sound. Most people are too intimidated or too lazy to express their opinions. Some are only subconsciously affected by something and couldn't enunciate their opinion even though their buying behavior is affected. Most companies count each customer complaint about a given product at 20 or 30 to 1, based on this premise. So the banker's notion about business leaders and neckties has much greater significance than just one solitary opinion from a banker with unfair preconceptions.

I do not like this fact, by the way. I wish image wasn't as important as it is. But fooling myself that way wouldn't be very smart. Comforting, but not smart. Comfortable, but not smart.

In Selling, We Succeed Based on What Is, Not on What Ought to Be

I agree that books should not be judged by their covers. People should not be judged by the clothes they wear or the length of their hair. I argued that point vehemently when I was young and my hair was long. But I also know that the reality is people do judge books and people by their covers.

I was at a social gathering this year and listened as the host's daughter, a recent high school graduate, complained bitterly to another guest, a doctor, about her experiences in the job market. She was dressed in a manner that can best be described as a cross between a hippie and a homeless person. The doctor asked if she had gone out seeking employment dressed that way.

"Of course!" she replied. In fact, she had gone to apply for a job behind the counter at a TCBY yogurt shop—where she would be greeting customers and serving food to them—and been told that she could not work there looking like that. "How dare they try to tell me how I can dress?" she demanded, outraged at the injustice of the world.

Sadly, she is not alone in her stupidity.

Would You Rather Be Right or Rich?

I chose the latter, and I've learned to package myself as appropriately and effectively as possible for various situations—to fit the costume to the role. I assure you that it does make a difference.

In my speaking activities, I've experimented and satisfied myself that I sell my educational materials to a higher percentage of an audience when I'm wearing a suit than when I'm wearing a sports coat and slacks. Also, there are clothes I might wear in

---

Dan Kennedy's #4
No B.S. Truth About Selling

The logic is simple: if the packaging of products
has an impact on how people regard those products,
then the packaging of people must have an impact
on how others regard those people.

California that I will not wear in Massachusetts, for example. I've learned these things make a dollars-and-cents difference in my results.

There is no doubt in my mind that the clothes and accessories you wear, the briefcase you carry, the pen you write with, and the car you drive all combine to communicate a message to others that can help you or hurt you. To deny it, to resist it, or to ignore it is self-destructive.

"Casual Friday" is a very bad idea for sales professionals. In fact, while I wouldn't suggest that you religiously adhere to everything as if it came from Moses chiseled in rock, I do suggest you read and carefully consider the information given in John Molloy's old *Dress for Success* books. Most of the advice is timeless.

Know this: people prefer dealing with successful people. I want my insurance agent, my real estate agent, my accountant, my lawyer, my doctor, and my public relations consultant to be doing well. The fact that they appear to be doing well indicates that many others agree with my choice and my judgment.

I've also observed that I'm treated with greater courtesy and respect by merchants, store clerks, waiters and waitresses, bank tellers, airline employees, and hotel clerks when I'm dressed for business than when I'm in casual clothes.

To be absolutely honest, I no longer live this advice day to day, but then I no longer sell much, given 90% of all my business is from continuing or repeat clientele, much of it done long-distance. I do dress casually when meeting with clients and running my coaching group meetings. I now live most of the time in a small town and spend as much time as possible around the racetrack with my horses, so comfortable jeans and boots are the order of the day. But if I am speaking to a new audience, I break out the pin-striped suit, tie, and cuff links. On the now rare occasion when I travel to a new client's offices, on goes the tie, gray or tan slacks, blue blazer. I have a separate section in the closet for my "selling wardrobe."

Penniless Immigrant Sells His Way to Wealth

My friend Nido Qubein is a case study in John Molloy-ish image.

Nido came here to go to college, barely speaking English, frequently confused by the language, with barely sufficient funds to get through school providing he also worked. He had no contacts, no assets, no advantages. Today, Nido is CEO of a growing national chain of more than 150 bread and baked goods stores, The Great Harvest Bread Company. He is on the board of directors of a bank, a highly paid professional speaker and consultant, and author of a number of books, including *How To Be a Great Communicator: In Person, On Paper and at the Podium*, which I suggest reading. I have known Nido for more than 20 years and watched his ascension to wealth, power, and significance. Without taking anything away from his acquired business acumen, expertise, diligent work, and other attributes or contributions to his clients, I think his success has as much or more to do with these two things than anything else: one, he is always impeccably dressed; and two, he is a masterful communicator and persuasive sales professional.

The joke at the National Speakers Association is that Nido is easy to find outside at the pool; he's the only one in the pool in a three-piece, pinstripe suit. I can't recall ever seeing him with so much as a wrinkle or crease; and I admit, I wonder how he does that, and I envy him his Cary Grant-like image.

Nido created his success by selling himself as an expert deserving exceptional compensation to executives at the highest levels when he was much younger, much poorer, and much less accomplished than they were. His "packaging" was vitally important. Yours might be too.

CHAPTER 6

Strategy 6
Remembering Why
You're There

This is an embarrassing confession.

One of the very first speaking engagements I ever had was for a client company at the opposite end of the country from my home. My compensation for speaking was to come solely from the sales of my books and cassettes to the audience; there was no fee being paid. Well, I went and spoke, and I was a hit! The audience laughed uproariously, applauded enthusiastically, even gave me a standing ovation at the end. I was back on the plane, halfway home, having a celebratory drink when it dawned on me that I had completely forgotten about the books and tapes hidden under the podium. I had forgotten to give my commercial, forgotten to sell anything, even forgotten to bring the product back with me. *I had forgotten why I was there!*

When Napoleon Hill, the author of *Think and Grow Rich,* wrote about "definiteness of purpose," he was surely aiming his remarks at those of us involved in sales and marketing. *Clarity of purpose* is very valuable and very important in advertising, sales, negotiation, and communication. You have to have a clear, single objective.

Many professional salespeople resist this idea and, as a result, never rise above mediocre performance levels. They argue that they have to be concerned with creating and sustaining goodwill, building rapport, developing a friendly relationship, gathering information, and a myriad of other things in addition to selling. Unfortunately, they use these other things as excuses for nonperformance, as camouflage for a real problem—such as the fear of asking for the order. Some salespeople muddle along as "professional visitors."

Dan Kennedy's #5
No B.S. Truth About Selling

A top performer in selling is always focused on selling. A successful person takes this attitude, as described by Zig Ziglar: you've got my money in your pocket, and I've got your product in my briefcase, and I ain't leaving until we make the exchange.

One of the people I made a point of studying, to bolster my persuasive skills in general and my ability to sell to groups from the platform in specific, was Glenn W. Turner, the very controversial founder of Koscot, a cosmetics company, and Dare to Be Great, a self-improvement training company. The two companies together attracted an estimated 500,000 people in just three years to pyramid selling operations—largely through his remarkably powerful speeches. At the time, Glenn Turner was an international phenomenon, receiving immense media attention.

Glenn Turner, by the way, has a speech impediment. He was then and still is pretty difficult to listen to. In his early days in selling, he even had trouble getting hired for straight commission to sell sewing machines door to door. Certainly, nobody would pick him as one of the most persuasive public speakers and salespeople of all time.

But there's a film of an old speech by Turner called "Challenge To America," in which he is speaking to an audience of distributors and prospective distributors for one of his companies. He looks right at them and at the camera and says: "It's a good thing I don't have a hold of you cause I'd reach in and extract that check right out of your pocket."

I often think about that piece of film as I enter a "get the check" situation. Is that too tough for you? Is that high pressure? That's the way you've got to be to get what you want.

If you worry too much about peripheral issues—such as being liked, loved, or even respected—or if you "buy into" the other person's problems too much, you'll have a lot of "friends" but not much money.

That's why I think that you've got to take the "hot," new sales training programs with a big, fat grain of salt. There are a lot of different approaches being promoted these days. There's nonmanipulative selling, nonconfrontational selling, consultative selling, no-closing selling, even sensitivity training for salespeople. Most of this seems to get translated to timidity in the field, and to quote Zig Ziglar again, "Timid salespeople have skinny kids."

Today, in teaching and in using Group Presentation Marketing, I often remind myself: "Remember why you're there." I don't care how much they laugh or applaud; whether or not I get a standing ovation is of minor importance. What counts (and all that counts) is the number of people who buy and the amount they buy. These are the real statistics, the real measurements of success.

In fact, I'll tell you a "secret" about speaking that very few pros like to admit: It's surprisingly easy to get an audience to laugh, to applaud, even to give a standing ovation. You can be a mediocre speaker and still engineer those results. So the speaker who takes great pride in "audience ratings" is either foolish or pretentious. In contrast, it's a lot harder to get 70%, 80%, even 90% of the people in an audience to reach into their pockets, pull out their hard-earned money, and spend it on your materials. You have to deliver a greater quantity of better quality information with greater skill and charisma in order to get those results than you do just to get applause.

For 10 of the 25 years of my speaking career, I appeared on publicly promoted seminar programs with Zig Ziglar and numerous celebrities in virtually every major U.S. and Canadian city. As the last speaker, I followed the last famous person and usually had the 5 to 6 P.M. or 6 to 7 P.M. time slot. The audience had been there since 7 or 8 A.M., sitting on hard bleachers or stadium seats in arenas. As I walked on stage, they were poised to leave. Yet, even under these challenging circumstances, I routinely sold $40,000.00 to $75,000.00 worth of my books and cassettes each and every time. How? Because I was totally focused on one objective and one objective only: making sales. Every word, every story in my presentation had been carefully chosen and assembled to make sales. The only measurement of my success I was interested in or paid any attention to was the number of sales.

Thinking It Over

The reason very few speakers ever become top performers in Group Presentation Marketing, why very few salespeople become high performers in their fields, is because they avoid putting themselves totally on the line for instant, measureable results. In the business of selling, the most significant sales are made after the seventh or eighth call-back to the customer or client. I say this has a lot more to do with the salesperson than with the customer. It is the salesperson's reluctance to push for definite results that causes this statistic.

In one of the monthly interview audiotapes I do for my Gold Inner Circle Members, I asked my Gold/VIP Member Dr. Charles Martin, a top cosmetic dentist often presenting treatment plans in the $30,000.00 to $70,000.00 range, how he responded to prospective patients who said they needed to go home and "think it over." After a moment's thought, he said if he heard that, it meant he had failed at his presentation. "When they say that, they mean they are going home and not coming back."

Most salespeople like to make themselves feel good by having a lot of "almost persuaded" prospects they're working on and calling back. But not me. I'd much rather have a *no* than a *maybe*. I'd rather know where I stand as quickly as possible, so that I can move on to the next potentially productive use of my time. When somebody says to me, "Let me think about it," I say:

- Let's think about it together, out loud. After all, two heads are better than one.
- What, specifically, do you need time to think about?
- When someone has to think over a decision like this, it usually means he or she doesn't yet have enough information with which to make a decision. Let's review what we do know to see what may be missing.

I push to get on with it, right then.

These days, in selling my own services as a speaker or as a consultant, as quickly as possible I open my schedule and say, "Let's see if I can even fit you in this month" or "Do you have a date in mind? Over half of mine for the rest of the year are already booked." I'm "closing" in this way from the very start.

Those who insist on thinking things over present to you just one more challenge: to determine whether or not you know why you're there and whether or not you're strong enough to get what you wanted. If you are clear on your purpose—for calling someone, meeting with someone, making a presentation—you'll have a big competitive edge over most of the rest of the world. Just having a clear agenda is a big step forward!

CHAPTER 7

Strategy 7
Do Expectations
Govern Results?

I t was a big surprise to me when I first discovered that many people actually go into situations expecting to lose.

My friend Brendan Suhr was an assistant head coach with Chuck Daly in the late 1980s when the Detroit Pistons were dominating the National Basketball Association. When Suhr was asked what the big difference was between the Pistons and other NBA teams, Brendan said that, unlike other organizations he'd been with, everybody with the Pistons genuinely and wholeheartedly *expected* to win every game.

I don't think most salespeople expect to "get the check" every time out. They expect to be put off, expect stalls, expect multiple meetings and presentations to be necessary, and generally expect NOT to get successful results—more often than not, they get what they expect.

I have been in those selling situations myself and with others; I have observed other people making excuses in advance for poor performance, and I always work very hard to stop myself from doing so. Even when going into "hostile territory" or difficult selling situations, I always figure out a strategy I can have confidence in and go in expecting to win.

A few years ago, I was referred to a Fortune 500 corporation to discuss taking on a complex advertising project for them. I was told by the executive who brought me in that the CEO, his vice president of marketing, and his ad agency folk who would be at the meeting all thought my kind of direct-response marketing was voodoo. I was told the CEO would never agree to my standard compensation, which adds royalties tied to results on top of fees. Frankly, most of the time, if I'm aware of such an unfriendly, ill-prepared environment, I simply refuse to go. Fortunately, I no longer need to try and convert the ignorant. But in this case, for several compelling reasons, I went. I could have gone in accepting the executive's cautions and either compromised my presentation and compensation demands or braced myself for failure. I did neither. I did my homework, researched the CEO's background, the company's situation, its competition, and went in with a strategy and information I felt would be compelling. And I walked out with $100,000.00. I intended nothing less.

About five years ago, I consulted with an industrial company with a sales force accustomed to six- to eight-month sales cycles, multiple meetings before closing a sale, and dealing with decisions by committees. They refused to hear the message that their extended sales cycle was the result of their own expectations. About a year later, I had the opportunity to consult with their chief competitor, a company half their size, experiencing the exact same frustrations but blessed with a relatively open-minded president and sales team. We designed a radically different "top down" marketing strategy targeting the CEOs of their prospect companies and intended to go from zero to a closed sale in a maximum of three meetings, three months. Over the past three years, this company has surpassed its competitor in sales and size and is averaging only 48 days from first contact to contract with new accounts.

This past year, my Gold/VIP Member Chris Mullins, who sells services to the health care, insurance, and hospitality industries, says she cut her sales cycle by half. How? By changing her expectation about how long it should take to close the sale, then re-engineering her pace of follow-up to match.

One more example: I'm told that in the real estate business, an ever-growing number of homeowners are meeting with three to five different agents before choosing one to list their home for sale. Thus, the average agent will close only 20% to 33% of listing presentations. My client and friend, Craig Proctor, consistently in the top ten REMAX agents worldwide (and a coach to thousands of other agents) consistently closes more than 90% of his listing presentations. His misses are rare. How can such a thing be possible? He expects it, so he has engineered a marketing and sales system to match that expectation. Doing so required ignoring industry norms—i.e., others' expectations—from the very beginning.

My speaking colleague Mike Vance, a former close working associate of Walt Disney, tells about asking the CEO of a company he was consulting to name his most vexing problem. Vance then asked, "Who's working on solving it?"

"No one, " answered the CEO, "because it cannot be solved."

Unfortunately, that attitude doesn't afflict only CEOs. It affects "stuck" sales managers and salespeople too.

Here's what I've come to devoutly believe: a marketing and selling system or process can be devised to achieve virtually any desired result or expectation. You start with the way you want things to occur, then work backward to put in place whatever is necessary to make it so.

Many people respond to an unsuccessful effort by saying, "I didn't expect that to happen anyway." I say, "Then why did you waste any effort on it? If you don't honestly expect success today, why not just roll over and go back to sleep?"

But let's be clear about this: I'm not talking about groundless, unreasonable expectations built out of "positive thinking" and nothing else. I'm talking about expecting success because you've created reasons to expect success.

Here's how I approach a selling or negotiating situation. First, I anticipate the worst—and carefully think through the

---

Dan Kennedy's #6
No B.S. Truth About Selling

Super-successful salespeople expect
successful results.

---

ways that I may be able to counter or overcome the predictable, possible obstacles. Then, I expect the best. Often, I visualize the entire process, rehearsing the entire dialogue in my head once, twice, even several times before actually proceeding with the meeting. I sell myself on the likelihood of getting what I want. And I believe this to be a vitally important sale to make.

These self-management techniques are from the previously mentioned Dr. Maxwell Maltz's *Psycho-Cybernetics*. And there is a Psycho-Cybernetics book specifically for sales professionals, *Zero Resistance Selling*.

About 15 years ago, I set out to sell a division of one of my companies to a competitor, and I used this process. Although I use the same process often, I mention this example because it involved difficult obstacles and circumstances. The business I wanted to divest was troubled, and that was no secret. There was the reasonable possibility the competitor could wait patiently and let us disappear from his landscape without giving us a penny. Our technology was antiquated. And I had no significant flexibility in price or terms; there was a number I had to have, and I had to be paid immediately.

I thought through all the reasons why it made good sense for them to accept the proposition—from their point of view. I thought through the possible reasons not to do the deal and developed answers to them. I played out the entire meeting in my imagination, what Dr. Maltz terms the "Theater of Your Mind." By the time I sat down with my competitors in the first meeting, I had every expectation of successfully consummating the deal. In fact, I was a little surprised when I walked out without a definite yes and had to wait a couple of weeks to complete the transaction.

Expectation is a powerful force. This concept is described by Napoleon Hill in his book *Think and Grow Rich*: "Whatever the mind of man can conceive and *believe*, it can achieve." (Emphasis is mine.)

Believe is the key word in this equation. You have to believe your proposition before anyone else will. And I am convinced that when your belief reaches 100%, you are guaranteed acceptance by the other person—the customer, client, whomever.

Persuasion involves transferring your feelings onto the other person. If you "secretly" feel

- I'm not very good at persuading others
- He's too smart to fall for this
- He'll never go for this
- He's a much better, much more experienced negotiator
- I wish this problem didn't exist with this deal
- I hope he hasn't gotten a quote from XYZ, because I can't beat their prices

then you'll "transmit" those feelings to the other person, and they could affect the response. He may become uncomfortable, hesitant, insecure, and reluctant to proceed, maybe without consciously knowing why, saying, "It's just a feeling."

On the other hand, when you feel

- The proposition is at least as good for the other party as it is for you
- The other person would be smart to say yes and stupid to say no
- You have something to offer that is better than anything available from any other source

- You are as good at communicating all of that as anyone could possibly be, you transfer those feelings, too.

Many professional salespeople with tremendous ability, extensive knowledge of their products, good selling skills, comprehensive training and education, and excellent opportunities repeatedly fail miserably. Why? Just one ingredient is missing in their situation: conviction—the belief in themselves and their proposition.

I'll say it again. This is the "magic promise" of virtually irresistible persuasive power: When your BELIEF reaches 100%, you are GUARANTEED ACCEPTANCE by the other person.

CHAPTER 8

Strategy 8
Proof: The Most Important Tool for Exceptional Success in Selling

I am about to reveal to you—and attempt to sell you on—the single most important, most powerful selling tool that exists. That's a big claim. I know that. Yet I have personally seen this single tool transform losing businesses into huge successes, and mediocre salespeople into superstars. I have used it myself many different times, many different ways, for great profit.

First, a story.

One afternoon I was visiting the offices of a famous, very successful criminal attorney. (By that, I do not mean he was a criminal. He represents people alleged to be criminals. Admittedly, a thin line.) He and several of his associates were gathered in the firm's conference room discussing a trial that was to begin the following day. He was asking his associates for their comments about their ability to win their client's acquittal.

The client had the risk of serving at least 20 years, possibly longer, in a federal prison should these lawyers fail. In the client's favor was the fact that this particular lawyer very rarely lost a case.

The attorney asked his associates for their comments, and a young lawyer spoke up: "I'm confident that we have gathered enough proof for you to prove his innocence if necessary."

The attorney came up out of his chair, lunged across the conference table, grabbed his young associate by the neck, and pulled him out of his chair, so that they were almost nose-to-nose. He then said, in a deadly voice: "Don't ever send me into a courtroom with 'enough' proof. I want a *preponderance* of proof."

I have never forgotten the importance of that lesson. Having a preponderance of proof makes it possible to sell with 100% effectiveness, 100% of the time. If you want to win with every presentation of every proposition, make sure you have an overwhelming *amount* of proof that what you are selling is a great deal, have an overwhelming *quality* of proof, and have proof that is influential.

Dan Kennedy's Definition

Preponderance of proof: An overwhelming quantity and quality of proof.

Proof through Testimonials

I have now done work with clients in 156 different product and service categories, from weight loss

---

and cosmetic dentistry to investments to funeral homes to cus-tom-fabricated parts for nuclear power plants. And I have yet to find one business—*not one*—where using testimonials as proof hasn't substantially improved sales. Yet 90% of all the sales pro-fessionals I encounter—those who try selling to me, those I am hired to observe and train, those who seek me out for assis-tance—either completely fail to use testimonials or use them sparingly and poorly.

If you did nothing else as a result of this book but increase by ten your use of testimonials in "proving your case" to your prospects, your reading time will produce a huge return on investment.

Testimonial letters and comments can be used in sales and marketing in many different ways. They can be used in advertis-ing, direct mail, and promotional literature. They can be used as part of a one-on-one or group sales presentation. They can be given to the client to read. They can be put in a big notebook and kept in the waiting room or reception area for people to browse through.

Dan Kennedy's #7 No B.S. Truth About Selling

What others say about you and your product, service, or business is at least 1,000 times more convincing than what you say, even if you are 2,000 times more eloquent.

In my experience, there is nothing more valuable than a great testimonial letter—other than two great testimonial letters!

At the end of this chapter, I've included one of the best demonstrations of truly powerful testimonials ever created by one of my Inner Circle Members. His name is Paul Johnson, and he owns Shed Shop Inc., a company with showrooms in several California cities, where they sell and build backyard sheds. This is a rather ordinary product made extraordinary through the emotional, human interest stories collected from satisfied customers and published in a booklet titled, *83 Practical Uses for a Shed Shop Shed* (see Figure 8.1). I originally suggested this to Paul as a *"Chicken Soup for the Shed Shop Owner's Soul"* type of story book, mimicking the hugely successful approach taken by my friend Mark Victor Hansen, co-creator of the best-selling phenomenon the actual *Chicken Soup for the Soul* book series. Paul executed the idea brilliantly. I'll let him tell you of the results in his own words:

> At a marketing conference for his Inner Circle Members in 1999, Dan was drilling into us the importance of using testimonials. I mentioned that our customers were always telling us interesting, unusual, even heart-warming stories about how they used our sheds, and Dan said I could do a book of them. And I did.
>
> To get the stories, we held a contest for the most creative or unusual use for a Shed Shop shed, invited our customers to submit stories and photos, and awarded prizes. We wound up with a booklet titled *83 Practical Uses for a Shed Shop Shed*, containing the 83 best stories.
>
> We send this booklet to every prospect. The impact was immediate and dramatic. Selling became much easier, as the

customers were presold on doing business with us and more eager to talk with us about why they wanted a backyard shed. This supported an increase in our prices, it sets us apart from competitors, it helps sell add-on options. I now think of it as my million-dollar storybook!"

This booklet has worked so well that Paul recently brought me in to produce a 30-minute infomercial-style videotape featuring a number of his testimonials, interviewed in their backyards, showing off their sheds.

Anyone can copy this "storybook idea," and many of my Inner Circle Members inspired by Paul's example have.

How Dumb Salespeople Work Ten Times Harder than They Need to and Get One-Tenth the Results They Could Get

If you underutilize testimonials, there you are, huffing, puffing, straining, spending, and struggling to convey your marketing message and convince would-be customers of your virtues, while you lock an entire army of better, more persuasive, more instantly believable salespeople eager to do the heavy lifting for you for free, bound, and gagged, locked in the closet, out of sight.

How dumb is that?

On the next page of this chapter, you will find a sign I gave to all my Gold Inner Circle Members back in 2002. It is copyrighted, but you have my permission to photocopy the page as much as you like for your own use or for others in your sales organization. Stick it up places you'll see it often to nag you as I would in person if I could.

"Let THEM Say It For You"

© 2002/D.S. Kennedy. www.dankennedy.com

A Picture Is Worth a Thousand Words

Another incredibly powerful type of proof is pictorial. The cliché is true: a picture is worth a thousand words. Pictorial proof is interesting and novel, it communicates at a glance, and it has lasting impact. Your camera could be your best friend in sales!

The late Ira Hayes, a former top National Cash Register (NCR) salesman, used this technique when he started selling cash registers to small shop owners. That was when the cash register was a new "technology," replacing the cigar box under the counter. Hayes had a 20-to-30-foot, black fabric panel that he carried with him. On that panel were thousands of snapshots of happy, satisfied customers standing next to their shiny, new cash register. Hayes would take this giant "wall" of snapshots into a prospect's office and unfurl it impressively. The sale was made before the selling even started—because the proof was overwhelming.

Ira was once asked, when he was traveling and speaking for NCR, why he and his company were so willing to reveal his selling secret. Ira answered, "We're not worried about our competitor's salespeople stealing this idea. We can't even get our own people to use it."

I've seen only one other salesperson use it to a similar extent: a Ford salesman in Phoenix. He is, in my opinion, the best, most professional automobile salesperson in the business—and I have met many others. In his cubicle, the walls are covered with snapshots, showing a customer or a customer-family, smiling, standing next to their new vehicle. Each photo is dated and has the customer's name on it. I am there with my Lincoln. My brother is there with his pickup truck. My father is there with his Mercury Marquis. Some families are there many times with a series of vehicles they have purchased over the years. It doesn't take too long to accept

Incidentally, I recently had reason to buy a Ford from another dealership in another state. I walked in and paid cash for a $35,000.00 SUV. I was never shown any testimonials, nor was I asked to give a testimonial or even a referral. And there has not been one ounce of follow-up from that sales rep. Next year, in that state, I'll buy two cars—neither one from him.

the pictures as proof that this guy treats his customers right—otherwise, how could he have so many of them?

You can use "photo proof" in any type of business. A retail store might take pictures of happy customers with their newly purchased merchandise. A lawn service company might photograph the customers' yards and gardens. A florist might photograph the happy, surprised recipients of delivered flowers. In my literature, I often use the photos taken of me with famous people: actors and actresses I've worked with in infomercials; athletes, coaches, even former U.S. presidents I've appeared with on seminar programs. Give some thought to how you can apply this principle to your business.

Statistical Proof

Statistics provide a third impressive form of proof. For example, I surveyed a group of entrepreneurs who were using my audio-cassette materials one year, and I've since shown the survey results to hundreds of audiences. The results show

- 98% reported satisfaction,
- 83% reported improved sales, and
- 87% made additional purchases.

At my suggestion, my client, Joe Polish, of Piranha Marketing, who works with carpet-cleaning industry business owners, surveyed a group of owners who attended his high-priced "marketing boot camp" a year afterward. From that survey, he documented that the owners achieved a $40,000.00 average income increase, which he was then able to use as a powerful sales tool for subsequent boot camps: "It's not costing you $3,000.00 to come; it's costing you $40,000.00 to stay home!" In one of the successful direct-mail campaigns I designed for this boot camp, we sent a very realistic faux check, made out to each prospect by name, for $40,000.00. Also enclosed was a form designed for the business owner and spouse to plan what they'll do with the extra $40,000.00.

To pile up more proof, three years ago, Joe began offering a "better your best" business contest to those using his systems, giving away a Jaguar, a Hummer, a Corvette, cash, and other prizes to the top achievers. As a result, he has thoroughly documented very specific improvements in hundreds of cleaners' businesses via the statistical reports, daily diaries, photos, and videos they submitted to compete in the contest. Just how powerful is all this? Well, at his most recent seminar, he sold more than $1.2-million in coaching programs from a 60-minute presentation.

How Much Proof Is Enough?
How Much Proof Is Too Much?

There is no such thing as enough; no such thing as too much. It is better to have more than you need rather than less.

I can't tell you how many salespeople and businesspeople I have taught this to, yet it is still a well-kept secret. No one else at the car dealership where the car salesman I described works will use the ideas, even though he has been a star, award-winning, high-income performer. Why not? Maybe other salespeople are lazy. Maybe they have low self-esteem that prevents them from excelling. Maybe they think the concept won't work in their line of work.

It's not your job, though, to worry about why others won't use these techniques. Their resistance is your opportunity! Successful people do the things that unsuccessful people are unwilling to do. If you choose to join the successful minority, you'll discover that most of the things you do to get results—even if openly shared

Other Proof

Consider these ideas for evidence you might use

Traditional

- Customer or client lists
- Length of time in business
- Past credentials, qualifications, experience
- Financial references
- Number of cities/countries serviced
- Number of customers served
- Physical demonstrations, "live" or on video
- "Flip books," binders, or PowerPoint presentations of testimonials used in face-to-face selling

Untraditional

- "Story books"
- Infomercial-style testimonial videos
- Audiotapes with testimonial interviews
- Toll-free 800-number "eavesdrop lines" to hear what clients or customers have called in and recorded about your product or service
- Testimonial letters, photos, etc., presented in a Web site

with others—will rarely be copied and used. For that reason, the use of *preponderance of proof* as the core of selling or advertising or marketing remains a best-kept, immensely valuable secret.

FIGURE 8.1: The Shed Stories

Living Room Saver
By Robert & Sue M. of San Jose

Our daughter moved back home with her infant son. She had a storage unit, but due to cost, she had to move her things out. Her stuff ended up in my living room. We seriously considered a huge bonfire, but we chose *The Shed Shop* instead. I wanted my living room back! Other sheds we looked at didn't seem to have the same high quality. We had to save up the extra money but it was worth it.

We now use it for holiday decorations and all our daughters household items. I was surprised when I finally got my living room back... I had forgotten the color of the carpet.

Junk Unworthy of New Shed
By Jim L. of San Carlos

Just wanted to drop you a note and tell you that the shed you installed for us last week has caused a lot of consternation between my wife and I.

We needed a shed to store all our tools, power mower, weed wacker, etc - you know, all the typical junk people throw into a normal shed. But, this shed (cottage) is WAY TOO NICE to clutter up with garbage! After painting and my wife putting flowers in the boxes it's so darn nice I want it for a nice, quiet place in the back yard to relax and listen to music. But no, my wife wants to fill it with junk! See what you have started! Please, go back to building the old aluminum or plastic tubs that look like outhouses and let my wife and I live in peace!

Yeah, it's a "cottage" ...

Tea Party Room
By Judy H. of Fremont

Al & I found ourselves with a partially enclosed shed with no door & a cement slab floor where water leaked in each winter. We knew we wanted a shed & looked at buying a metal shed...also looked at other wood sheds. *The Shed Shop* sheds were far superior.

After our shed was installed, we had it painted the same color as our house. I also added shutters and a flower box. We put linoleum on the floor, and added two heavy duty shelves. In addition we have a locked metal cabinet for our paints and other toxic items. The final touch was to add a workbench that looks out one of the windows over the garden.

However, the most unique use I have found for the shed is for my annual tea party. I have six great nieces and each year for the past three years I have hosted a tea party. Part of the festivities involve dressing up in party dresses, old hats, high heels, etc. This year the tea party "shed" became Noah's Ark. No entrance was allowed, what with the lions, tigers, etc. The kids did get to pet the elephants, and a grand time was had by all. Who knows what next year brings!!!

I've had so many compliments on the shed and it has been a joy to work and play in. Perhaps the most surprising thing is it stays relatively cool on warm days and relatively warm on cool days...all with no insulation. We're looking forward to many more years of use and to many more tea parties.

FIGURE **8.1:** The Shed Stories, continued

Singer's Studio
By Gary M. of Grizzly Flats

My wife, Jackie and I are both singers (we met as members of the Northern CA Vocal Artists Association). Our karaoke equipment, including hundreds of background tapes, had not had a separate room since we moved to Grizzly Flats in September 1996. The equipment was in our bedroom. Our guest room and our office were too small and adding another room onto the house would have been far too costly.

A separate shed was the ideal solution as it provides for a designated room and we don't bother our 8-year-old daughter Tabby. In comparing *The Shed Shop* with other companies it was clear *The Shed Shop* was the best. Even though it was the most expensive, the quality of your shed more than made up for this "negative."

We had a contractor put in electricity, insulation, and walls. We have all of our equipment, tapes, and CD's in the shed in addition to music-related pictures on the walls.

I'm singing my 50's-60's rock-n-roll and Jackie her show and other songs. It's great! Should we get more than one room full of company, the futon in the shed will sleep 2 adults or 3-4 children. I can also see patients there if anyone wants to come to Grizzly Flats (I'm a psychotherapist). My satisfaction has been complete thus far.

Singin' in the trees...

Parental Storage
By Julie N. of Alamo

A move from Idaho resulted in a smaller house & garage but a bigger fixer-upper yard. Storage was very tight. An old shed served only to house black widows & stray rain drops. Anything in the old shed turned green and mushy.

Other alternatives included an expansion of the garage... impractical & expensive. *Shed Shop* sheds were charming and priced right. Customer service was great... knowledgeable, quick & efficient. I wish all California builders were this good! Do you do houses??

Our new shed houses garden equipment; saddles I will never part with...despite what my husband says; dog houses that the new dog will not enter. I even kidded with my parents I would store them in there when they "retired." They were OK with that because it is so cute.

It has become "yard art!!" We jazzed it up with antique accents. It adds charm to our views. We even planted our shed its own cute little garden.

Mom & dad's retirement home?

FIGURE **8.1:** The Shed Stories, continued

Computer Room
By Lisa D. and family of Livermore

Just wanted you to see another variation on your wonderful sheds. My family and I have converted it into a computer room to free up a bedroom for our new baby boy.

We all spend most evenings in here and are surprised at how roomy and comfortable it is. We currently house 3 computers (9 hard drives total), a TV, 3 VCR's, a scanner, 2 printers, a fax machine and MORE. And it all fits so nicely in 120 square feet.

All of our friends think it's great! And we saved about $50,000 dollars when compared to a room/house addition! We have had no problems with our shed. Thanks again for a wonderful product!

Peanut Shack
By Don S. of San Jose

Our shed is a multipurpose building that houses old paint, sprayers, teak furniture, and peanuts for visiting squirrels. It definitely holds more peanuts for my squirrels than I realized! We are 100% satisfied with *The Shed Shop.*

For visiting squirrels...

Recreational Equipment Filled My Garage
By Dave C. of Palo Alto

Our garage was crowded with all your typical outdoor stuff...bikes, skateboards, roller blades, & other recreational equipment. Not enough room left for the cars!!

We tried garage organizers, shelving, storage hooks, etc. But it was still crowded and difficult to access both the equipment and cars.

I chose *The Shed Shop* over others due to: 1) quality design/materials/construction; 2) friendly staff; 3) ability to have shed built-to-order; 4) ability to drive & see samples on their lot. It now houses all our outdoor stuff.

While your prices weren't the lowest, this was the best value: quality, attractive, great team. I've recommended you to several friends & neighbors!!

Cars In, Filing Cabinets Out!
By Terri C. of San Ramon

My home business requires that I keep client files from prior years in my garage in 4 filing cabinets. When we bought a new car, we needed to now park our 3 cars in the garage...the filing cabinets needed to go!

To solve the problem, we chose a shed from *The Shed Shop* for their great looks and sturdy construction. The shed is easily seen by our neighbor so we didn't want to create an eyesore for them. The filing cabinets are now in the shed as are our earthquake supplies & water.

As a joke to one neighbor (who has no shed), another neighbor (who also has a shed) and I hung Christmas lights on our sheds in July. Our "in-between" neighbor really enjoyed the festive look of the shed & we all had a good laugh.

FIGURE **8.1:** The Shed Stories, continued

Workshop and Storage
By Yolanda P. of San Lorenzo

We had an old metal shed in the back yard that was too small and was falling apart, it was rusting away. For two years things were piling up in the garage and patio area. There was no other alternative to getting a new shed. We just had to decide what size, when to purchase, and who to buy it from. Once we visited *The Shed Shop* and saw some of the displays, we were totally convinced that this was the way to go.

Our new shed is being used as a work shop and storage area. A work bench has been built and shelf installed in the shed. Some of the stored items include fishing rods, camping equipment, and mountain bikes. With the new shed our garage and patio area is neater and cleaner looking. Your people did a great job from start to finish, keep up the good work.

Great use of wall space!

Santa's Workshop
By Karen W. of Redwood City

Our garage had been turned into our family room years ago and storage space has always been a huge problem. I liked the looks of a wooden structure in the yard since it is readily seen from the house.

I plan to decorate the shed at Christmas as Santa's Workshop. My husband does look like Santa, too! We're using it for storage of all kinds of supplies, extra Costco purchases, Christmas tree and other holiday decorations. I didn't expect it to be such an addition to the looks of the yard - see picture.

Family Heirloom
By Dale, Nancy, & Kelsey S. of Fremont

Last spring we visited some model homes in Sacramento and in one of the backyards there was a little playhouse set up. Our daughter Kelsey fell in love with it and all she could do was talk about how "cool" it was. We had previously thought about getting her a playhouse, but decided we didn't want to spend that much money for something she would outgrow in a few years.

Then we heard about *The Shed Shop*. Here was a product that looked cute enough for a playhouse, yet could be used as a storage shed when Kelsey outgrew it. When we stopped in, a very nice woman explained everything about the sheds and what options were available. We decided on an extra window, dutch door, and flower box.

We wrapped up a *Shed Shop* brochure in half birthday and half Christmas paper and gave it to Kelsey at dinner. The look on her face was priceless. While waiting for the delivery date she talked non stop about all she would doing in it. She picked out paint colors (yellow, purple, and green), curtains, house numbers, mailbox, park bench, bookshelf, welcome mat, and carpet.

Kelsey has spent many hours in the playhouse using her imagination and having fun. We're sure as she grows the playhouse will be changed from a home for her dolls into a teenage refuge full of beanbag chairs and boomboxes. We hope this playhouse will be part of our family forever. We imagine our grandchildren coming to visit someday and telling them about the fun we had with their mom putting the playhouse together...and then watching them play in it too.

CHAPTER 9

Strategy 9
Fred Herman's
K.I.S.S. Principle

arl Nightingale once called the late Fred Herman "America's greatest sales trainer." It's a title I think he deserved. To my knowledge, Fred is the only salesman ever to appear as a guest on *The Tonight Show* with Johnny Carson. (Carson said, "OK, since you're the greatest salesman, sell me this ashtray." Fred picked it up, examined it, and asked, "If you were going to buy this ashtray, what would you expect to pay for it?" Carson named a price. Fred said, "Sold!")

I discovered Fred Herman's work after I already had years of experience in selling; I wish I had found it when I started. Fred is probably most famous for coining the KISS Principle for Selling:

Keep It Simple, Salesman! This is an immensely valuable lesson that I learned the hard way.

In my first sales position, with the publishing company I described earlier in this book, one of the spots where I was most effective was opening new accounts where we could place the entire six-foot-tall spinner rack. The standard procedure prescribed by the company was to review the catalog of books with the buyers so they could choose the titles to be displayed in the rack. As the rack held only about one-third of all the available titles, this selection process was a time-consuming chore. The customer and I had to discuss just about every title. Inevitably, he wanted more variety than the rack could accommodate. I found it took almost two hours, on average, to place a new rack.

Then I realized that almost 90% of the racks I placed carried the same titles. So I reasoned that I knew better than the customers which titles would sell best and that I was wasting their time and mine discussing products that would not be on the rack. From this realization, I created a "standard rack assortment," which I copied and used every time I sold a new customer a rack. All the customer had to do was initial the precompleted form, and I was on my way. Average time savings: 90 minutes per new rack placement!

How come nobody else in the company had thought of this?

People have an incredible tendency to complicate their lives. I'm not sure why that happens, but I know that it happens. I even have a name for it: complexity creep. Complexity just creeps up on you when you're not looking. And, unnecessary complexity creates a whole host of problems. It wastes time, it drains your energy and enthusiasm and it often confuses the customer. And confused customers do not buy!

You Can Get Rich Making the Complicated Simple

I recently saw an interesting advertisement placed by a copywriter looking for work. He billed himself as a "professional explainer" who specialized in "making complicated things simple and easy to understand." That's exactly what you need to do in your efforts to persuade others. (Too bad there's nobody who'll do that for me with assembly directions for things I buy or for my damned computer.)

Not long ago, I was wrestling with a direct-mail project involving the sale of a rather complicated financial product to essentially unsophisticated investors. Two consecutive test mailings failed miserably. I thought they were well-written, clear, and exciting. I thought they offered a great deal to the customer. I thought everything was right. Just one small problem: they didn't work. I read through them a hundred times and still found no clue to the problem. One evening, I got the idea to add a little diagram at the end of the literature that showed—in cartoon form—the gist of the product. The addition of this little drawing, which showed visually what was said in the copy, made the piece a huge success. The mailing with the drawing got phenomenally good results. That one little drawing made the complicated simple and understandable.

P.T. Barnum once said, "No man ever went broke overestimating the ignorance of the American public." Maybe that judgment of the American consumer is a little harsh, but it does introduce a major mistake made by the majority of sales and marketing people over and over again: overestimating the sophistication of their customers.

It's natural for you to insist that the people you deal with are smarter than everybody else's customers. That reflects well on

you, doesn't it? It's good for your ego to think that you're dealing with a "better class" of people. It may be good for the ego, but
it's bad for the bank account! Here is the best way to succeed in
advertising, selling, marketing, or persuading others (regardless
of who they are or how smart and sophisticated you believe they
are): present *everything* in the simplest possible language and in
the simplest possible form.

Close the Doors on the Sales Prevention Department

A lot of companies have a more active Sales Prevention
Department than they do a sales operation—overrun with sales-
killing policies, rules, laws, forms. Often this happens if the
lawyers and bean-counters gain excess power back at the home
office. I do not envy those of you working for the worst of these.
My first and only sales job mentioned earlier in this chapter was
with a company who had such a department, but even more so,
had management focused on everything but the ease and simplic-
ity with which an account could be opened and a new customer
brought into the fold. I was able to circumvent the home office
and invent my own streamlined, simplified sales process. Maybe
you can too. But if you must try dragging the powers-that-be
above you out of the sales prevention mode, here's a story that
may help you sell your ideas. Feel free to use it as your own.

I sometimes eat breakfast at a little, neighborhood, mom-
and-pop coffee shop near my home. There on the counter next to
the cash register sit three different receptacles for charitable
donations of coins—one for Kiwanis, one for some organization
for the blind, one for disabled veterans. One morning, as I

dropped my change into one of the receptacles, it registered with me that I always plunked my change into the same one. Why? I stood there for a few minutes, pondering my own behavior.

Then it hit me. The reason I *always* put my change into the disabled veterans jar was

- NOT because I had any preference for that charity over the others
- NOT because of any reasoned decision to support it instead of the others
- NOT because of the graphic design or appearance of the different containers
- NOT because of any sales copy on the containers
- NOT because of their arrangement on the counter.
- NOT for any thoughtful or logical or admirable reason

The reason, and the only reason, I put all my change into only one of these charity jars, each and every time, is because *the hole in the top of my favored jar is bigger than the holes in the lids on the other two jars.*

CHAPTER 10

Strategy 10
Sell Money
at a Discount

When you fully understand the technique of selling money at a discount and can find a way to apply it to your product, service, or business, you will have created a bottomless gold mine! (I'll admit, though, that it's not the easiest technique to apply universally.)

I was once retained as a consultant to an individual who lectured on methods of preventing theft from employees and vendors' delivery staff. This individual was a reformed thief who knew how it was done because he had done it. (This kind of theft is a little-known problem of huge magnitude. In the typical convenience store, for example, theft equals or even exceeds the owner's profit.)

This expert ex-thief was teaching business owners how to prevent this sort of loss—and they were thrilled. In fact, he had boxes full of testimonial letters from store owners and executives citing specific amounts of money saved in the weeks or months following his seminar. These letters documented savings of thousands of dollars per store. Some big companies reported saving as much as $100,000.00 in just a couple of months by applying what they learned.

But the thief-turned-consultant had no idea what he was worth. He was charging only $500.00 to conduct his all-day seminar, and he had one little reference notebook with six audio cassettes that recapped the seminar, simply packaged in a bag, that he was selling for about $30.00.

Let me confess: this was the easiest marketing task I ever had. The first thing I suggested was that he raise his fees. In fact, I convinced him to triple his fee from $500.00 to $1,500.00 immediately. To his shock (but not mine), there was very little protest and no loss of clients. Shortly after that, the fee was raised again to $2,500.00 with just a little client grumbling. Even at $2,500.00 a day, he was such a bargain that no one could afford to grumble too much. In essence, we were now selling $10,000.00 to $100,000.00 cash for $2,500.00. Who wouldn't buy that? And we had the proof to demonstrate the value of this bargain. Within a year, the consultant's fee was $7,500.00, and he was still attracting more business than he could handle.

I based his entire marketing program on *proving that he was offering money at a discount*. In other words, we showed prospects such a large, compelling return on investment that they couldn't say no, regardless of the price of the seminar.

In a previous chapter, I told you how Joe Polish proved he was selling $40,000.00 for $3,000.00 at his "marketing boot

> # Dan Kennedy's #8
> # No B.S. Truth About Selling
>
> In persuading others to part with their money,
> your best possible approach is to demonstrate
> that the apparent expense is not an actual expense
> at all but that what is being purchased is either
> free—or better yet—actually pays.

camps" for carpet-cleaning industry business owners. So you can see how this technique can work for consultants offering educational seminars.

In addition, there are numerous consultants in the fields of real estate mortgages, office leases, utility bill auditing, and freight cost reduction who guarantee to help clients save at least $10,000.00, and require fees of only $1,000.00 to $2,000.00 or a percentage of monies saved. Well, who wouldn't agree to that deal?

That's the kind of money-at-a-discount "picture" you somehow have to engineer and present for your product or service. The same basic principle applies to negotiating other types of financial transactions. You can sell just about anything if you can show the buyer how the *thing* (not the buyer) pays for the purchase; how the thing is, in effect, free.

You may never come across a situation where that demonstration is as clear-cut as it was with my client in the theft control business. I know I haven't come across another such situation. But the technique can be applied, to some degree, to most businesses. It may take some long, hard thought, some research, and some patience, but I assure you it's worth all that and more.

How to Put Money in Their Pockets and Then Set It on Fire

You've undoubtedly heard the saying "his money's burning a hole in his pocket." It's used to describe people who can't keep their hands off their money; they can't wait to spend it. I've done a lot of selling by first putting money in the prospect's pocket, then setting it on fire. You can too. Let me explain.

I sold millions of dollars of cassette learning systems to doctors in evening seminars; the seminars were free, but the doctors had to post a $25.00 deposit to guarantee they would show up. The deposit was "refundable" at the end of the seminar. After presenting the "commercial" and closing the sale, I'd do a "Columbo"— a sales technique named after the rumpled raincoat-clad character played by Peter Falk and famous for saying, "Just one more thing…." I would say,

> Oh, just one more thing, you'll recall you paid a $25.00 deposit to guarantee you'd be here this evening, and you've kept that promise, so your $25.00 *is* refundable. And we'll double that refund right before your very eyes; we'll match it with $25.00 of our money, so you can deduct $50.00 from your system purchase this evening. Just cross out the $499.00 price, deduct the $50.00, and write $449.00 on your form.

Even with an audience that many would argue was too sophisticated for such a strategy, this worked magically. What I did was put $50.00 into their pockets and then set it on fire. If they didn't buy a system, they "lost" that $50.00, and that hurt!

I've replicated this strategy in other group sales situations, in person-to-person selling, even in direct-mail campaigns.

General Motors and Ford are using a version of this idea with their "private label" Visa and MasterCard. You accumulate "rebate dollars" for using the card, but those dollars are good only toward the purchase of a vehicle. If you use that one Ford or GM Visa or MasterCard for all your credit card purchases, you might accumulate $2,000.00 to $3,000.00 in "rebate dollars." With that money burning a hole in your pocket, is there any way you'll "lose it" and buy another brand of car? I don't think so.

Becoming an "Added-Value" Sales Professional

Many sales professionals feel challenged by commoditization, and in some fields, price shopping facilitated by the Internet has worsened the situation, or at least their perception of the situation.

A few years ago, I spoke at the Advertising Specialty Institute's national convention, a congregation of all the people who sell imprinted giveaway items like pens, litter bags, snow scrapers, key chains, etc. I opened my talk with this statement:

"If you are in a commodity business, get out."

Afterward, I got a lengthy, outraged letter from one attendee who accused me of being a lazy idiot who hadn't bothered to gain any understanding of their business and had insulted all participants by telling them to get out of business.

She missed the point.

Someone who did get the point was one of my Gold/VIP Members, Mitch Carson of Impact Products, who has a thriving, growing ad specialty, premium, and promotional items business. He recognizes that their business is commoditized, that the "trinkets" can be easily price-shopped, and that to prosper, he must focus on bringing "added value" to clients. He has done that numerous ways—from designing year-long, multistep, multimonth customer retention and reward programs for businesses to customizing trinket-based promotions for certain industries, such as the Mother's Day cultured pearl promotion he built for restaurant owners. Carson also adds value by offering consulting and even by creating a comprehensive do-it-yourself promotion kit and getting into the information business. He now speaks at conferences and conventions and attracts clients from all over the country rather than just in his local area.

Another Gold Member in virtually the same business, Rel Luttrell, has niched himself to the banking industry, bundling promotional products with complete marketing or client retention/reward programs.

Yet another of my Gold/VIP Inner Circle Members, B. Shawn Warren, is in the exact same business; he markets imprinted specialty items. However, he has niched only to fraternal organizations and delivers a big cafeteria of "added value," including a how-to newsletter on leadership, custom pin designs by an inhouse artist, and an online "store" of in-stock, instant-ship items for most major fraternals.

Another of my Members, a private client who asked not to be named, is a very successful financial advisor who targets only owners of businesses, with $5 to $15 million of investable assets and family succession issues within their businesses. He hosts quarterly three-day mastermind meetings exclusively for his clients where he brings in top attorneys, psychologists, authors, and experts in family businesses. He says to his clients: "No other financial advisor will bring you together with 50 to 100 other family business owners in similar financial situations, to network, share ideas, advise each other, even identify profitable strategic alliance opportunities."

Creating Added Value from Thin Air

When I sell my cassette learning systems that have to do with advertising and marketing, as well as my Inner Circle Memberships, I always include several "critique coupons" that entitle the person to send me their ads, brochures, or sales letters for my personal, written minireport: an analysis of what they've done effectively and what could be done better. This is called a "second opinion consultation," for which I usually charge $100.00 to $200.00, depending on the complexity of the piece being reviewed. In other words, each of these coupons has a minimum value of $100.00. With a learning system that I sell at many seminars for $278.00, I include three coupons, so the customer gets $300.00 of added value with a $278.00 purchase. (A voided sample of the coupon, Figure 10.1, is shown at the end of this chapter.)

Creating Added Value at Nominal Cost

One of the benefits provided by the Internet is unlimited "library space" at virtually zero cost. My Gold, Gold+, and Gold/VIP Inner Circle Members have access codes for a restricted Web site filled with archives of my past *No B.S. Marketing Letters,* transcripts of my Marketing Gold audiotape interviews with top advertising, marketing, and sales experts; articles; and other resources. The content on this site expands and grows more valuable every month. It is significant added value to Inner Circle Members yet costs nearly nothing to provide.

Many businesses can and do use this idea. In my Membership, I know of attorneys, CPA's, chiropractors, ad specialty salespeople, insurance sales professionals, brokers, a manufacturer supplying the pharmaceutical industry, and dozens of others who provide useful collections of information only to their customers through restricted-access Web sites.

You can create added value through premiums, guarantees and warranties, special services, frequent-user rebates, club memberships—turn your imagination loose and find an opportunity that matches your particular business. (See Figure 10.1.) Added value allows you to make your "core" goods or services "free."

FIGURE **10.1:** Promotional Coupon

$100.00 Critique Certificate $100.00

Entitles bearer to submit any single printed piece;
brochure; catalog; direct-mail piece; advertisement or similar
promotional material by mail for critique by Dan S. Kennedy.

———————————

Send Certificate and Materials to:

Dan S. Kennedy
Kennedy Inner Circle, Inc.
5818 N. 7th St., #103
Phoenix, AZ 85014

Terms and Conditions

Certificate expires 12 months from date of purchase. Allow 4 to 6 weeks for Mr. Kennedy's response. Do NOT telephone; consultation given by mail only. Actual finished materials or "rough sketch" and copy for planned material may be submitted. Coupon redeemable only for listed services. Additional consulting may be contracted for, Mr. Kennedy's schedule permitting; fees quoted on request.

Please be advised that any materials submitted for review by Dan Kennedy, including those submitted with critique coupons, may be published in any of Dan Kennedy authored/edited publications, as examples. Also, submitted materials will not be returned. Do not submit materials you are concerned about keeping confidential.

© 2002/Kennedy Inner Circle

CHAPTER 11

Strategy 11
Always Compare
Apples to Oranges

"You can't compare apples to oranges." I'm sure you've heard that; I encourage you to get it completely out of your mind! The secret to eliminating price resistance *is* to compare apples to oranges! Let me give you an example:

From 1983 to 1987, I built the largest integrated publishing and seminar business exclusively serving chiropractors and dentists in North America. In my seminars for SuccessTrak Inc., I sold a 12-month "trak" (subscription) of audiocassettes on practice promotion and success subjects. Counting the bonus items, the one-year program included 18 cassettes and sold for $499.00.

But most audiocassette albums, available on a variety of topics, sell for an average of $10.00 a tape. On that basis, these 18 cassettes would sell for only $180.00. The economics of marketing via free seminars required that we sell for the considerably higher price. Also, due to the specialized, valuable nature of the information in these cassettes, we felt justified in commanding the higher price. But how do you clearly and successfully justify that price to the consumer? Obviously, if you compare other cassette products to these cassette products (apples to apples), you're dead.

In this case, we compared cassettes to seminars. If the participants obtained the same basic information in the cassettes by attending the seminars on which the cassettes were based, they would spend more than $780.00 on enrollment fees alone, not to mention time away from their practices during the week or family on weekends, travel and lodging costs, and other expenses. All things considered, by buying the tapes, people could save much more than $300.00!

By switching to an apples-to-oranges comparison, I presented a compelling argument of savings to the consumer.

Most of the Advice You Get About Dealing with Price Resistance Is Wrong

If you deal with price resistance by arguing in favor of your higher quality, your better service, etc., you will find your sales work difficult most of the time. People do want superior quality goods and services, but they still don't enjoy paying premium prices for them. Many marketers fight that battle unnecessarily.

It is much easier and much more effective to switch the standards of comparison. Win by comparing apples to oranges and then "throw in" the superior quality at "no extra cost."

If you are in a selling situation where there is headon competition, even competitive bidding, this technique can still be used. Recently I was consulting with a manufacturing company in direct competitive bid warfare with a lower-price opponent. My client was losing bid after bid. I said, "Something has to change here." They said, "It can't. We can't cut our prices any lower." I said, "if we can't come in with the lower bid, we might as well come in with an even higher bid— but let's change the rules of the game when we do it." They began changing the specifications for the bids, adding value, bundling goods and services together, extending warranties, and including delivery and completion guarantees. Then we built a "How to Compare Our Bid with Others Checklist." When it was all said and done, my client started

In my annual Renegade Millionaire Seminar (www.renegade millionaire.com), I teach people to "reinvent" their products and services so that they make direct price comparisons impossible. The smart sales pros step back from day-to-day activities, mentally take very deep breaths, and are able to look at their products or services with fresh eyes. The super-astute sales pros re-invent what they are selling altogether so that price comparison is impossible, the kind of added values discussed in the previous chapter are emphasized, customers or clients become "members," and the salespeople are positioned as specialists and expert advisors rather than salespeople. Ultimately, they get to sell in a competitive vacuum.

getting projects the company had been losing to low bidders before.

The savvy sales pro learns to alter the rules of the game to gain an overwhelming advantage. Forget all about "playing fair." Forget all about competing on a "level playing field." These are clichés that are best lasered out of your consciousness. All your life, you've been told to "play fair," and that conditioning of your subconscious may be holding you back now. Selling in competitive situations is all about finding or inventing an *unfair* advantage for yourself. Go ahead and make it impossible for your competitors to keep up with you.

That's exactly the approach I took with this client. I analyzed their operations and discovered that they were in a position to include warehousing and fulfillment at a much lower cost than their competitor could possibly do. By adding that service to their specifications, their higher quote became the most attractive quote.

Many big companies have learned this lesson, although they don't capitalize on it to the extent they could. In traveling, for example, I prefer to stay in an Embassy Suites if available. These are two-room suites with free cocktails and a free, full breakfast "built into" their room rates. In reality, their suites aren't much bigger than a full-size hotel room; they've just creatively apportioned and partitioned the space. By changing the standards of comparison, though, they have a product that is much more attractive to many people than their competitors. They have created a suite versus a room at a comparatively similar price.

There are many different ways to change the rules of the game and use apples-to-oranges comparisons. I urge you to look for ways appropriate to your selling activities. This is the price resistance eliminator!

CHAPTER 12

Strategy 12
In Search of
the Free Lunch

There's an old story about the king who commissioned a group of the brightest scholars in his kingdom to assemble the wisdom of the ages. They first came back with a truckload full of stone tablets. He told them to condense and simplify. They came back with an encyclopedia. He demanded that they condense and simplify. Finally, ultimately, they returned with a single sentence: there's no such thing as a free lunch.

Every sane, sensible logical person knows that to be the truth. However, we all still love to believe there might be! That's why premiums work so well in selling. A premium is a free gift or a free bonus: something the buyer gets free when purchasing something else. Everything from books to Buicks have been given away at one time or another as a premium with a purchase. I personally love to use premiums in selling.

When I was consulting with a publishing company, I put together a direct-mail campaign for a line of their programs with the theme "Success comes in cans, not in cannots." For the premium, we offered a little baby food can with the "Success

Tips for Using Premiums

- Don't give away the same things you sell. In most cases, this is a bad practice because it devalues your merchandise or services.

- Offer premiums that people want for themselves. Even if you're in the business-to-business marketing environment, it's best to offer a luxury personal-use item.

- Give away things people want but rarely buy for themselves. I've found that people will often buy something as a premium that they ordinarily would never buy on its own.

- Make the premium relevant to your offer or to your customers or clients.

comes in cans" label. The campaign was extremely successful, which I am certain had much more to do with the customers' desire for the premium than for the product. Consider the following:

- More than 80% of the customers ordering by phone made a point of asking about the premium to make sure they would get it.
- More than 30% of the purchasers asked about getting extra "cans" for friends or associates.
- A large number of inquiries were received from people who wanted to buy the can labels but not the programs advertised in the mailing.

It goes to show that people do respond to desirable premium offers, and premiums can even drive the sale.

How to Close the Difficult Sale with a Very Desirable Premium

For many years, the direct selling companies in the home security and fire alarm systems businesses have relied on desirable premiums. Although everybody needs and should have a fire alarm system in their home, nobody wants one, and so it is a difficult sale. Typically, these companies will offer a beautiful set of crystal and dinnerware, or a gorgeous collection of jewelry, or an all-expenses-paid vacation as the free bonus gift to close the sale. This lets the buyers get something they really want while doing the right thing and purchasing something they really need. The gift may very well be something they would never buy for themselves, but they love the opportunity of getting it "free."

How to Strengthen Customer Retention and Stimulate Referrals with Premiums

Premiums can also be used to improve customer retention and stimulate word-of-mouth advertising. When my favorite car salesman delivered the last Lincoln Continental I bought, he called my attention to a little Auto Butler decal on the window. Any time during the first year I had the car, if I had a flat tire, dead battery, locked my keys in the car, or had some other problem, I could call the Auto Butler and they would come fix the problem—free. This was not promised to me as an inducement to buy the car; I didn't find out about it until he delivered the car. But I've since told at least a dozen people about it. Why? Like anybody else, I like to brag about getting a good deal.

You can implement some sort of program on your own as well. My chiropractor has a wall display featuring several different health products, a popular exercise device, even a package of movie tickets. You can choose one as your gift when you refer two patients to the practice. Does it work? Fabulously well.

Premiums and "Big-Ticket Selling"

You can even use premiums in negotiating. With one big consulting contract I closed, I "threw in" a complete library of my books and audiocassette programs. The retail value was well over $2,500.00, but the cost to me was less than $300.00. I once gave away a certain amount of consulting time to an individual, for his business as a "bonus" for his investing in one of my companies. In selling a business, I included consulting time as a bonus. I know a businessman who secured the services of a top lawyer by including free use of a private plane in addition to the normal retainers and fees.

My Gold/VIP Member Al Williams, a commercial mortgage broker dealing exclusively with commercial real estate agents handling large apartment building transactions, periodically gives away a Palm Springs golf resort vacation to the broker bringing him the most business—highlighting this in his direct-mail has brought many new brokers to him.

Another client of mine, who asked not to be named, provides investment-related services to affluent M.D.s and surgeons. His "new client welcome gift" is a week's stay in the luxury beachfront condominium he owns in the Bahamas. He vacations there himself 4 weeks a year, leaving 48 weeks to give away to new clients.

You can use the "free lunch technique" many different

You are well aware of "frequent buyer" reward programs, modeled after the airlines' frequent flyer programs. But you don't have to be a big business to use such a strategy. The publisher of my *No B.S. Marketing Letter* is Bill Glazer, a very successful owner of independent retail stores, and a marketing "guru" in retailing. He has developed a turnkey, easy-to-implement rewards program now used by thousands of retailers, service businesses, and other types of businesses, as part of his comprehensive system for locking in customers, stimulating more frequent purchases, larger purchases, and referrals. You can get information about his entire system, and the rewards program specifically, from www.bgsmarketing.com.

ways in business. Do not make the mistake of overlooking or discounting the powerful and universal appeal of this approach.

The Remarkable Strategy of "Gift-with-No-Purchase"

OK, everybody's heard of gift-*with*-purchase, and I've now given you numerous examples of that strategy successfully applied. Now let me tell you about gift-with-*no*-purchase, a strategy I've applied in the mortgage industry, with my friend Tracy Tolleson, with such amazing success that he and I are now licensing the entire "system" we built to one mortgage broker or loan officer per city, at approximately $25,000.00 per license.

Tracy is a very successful, high-income, but incredibly lazy residential mortgage broker in Phoenix. I say "lazy" in a good way! He likes to play a lot of golf; he insists on doing business on his terms, at his convenience (and you can read a lot more about that in my *No B.S. Time Management* book); and he never, ever, ever cold-calls prospects, so he must get business flowing to him. He also prefers dealing with real estate agents who bring him new purchases to finance rather than directly with consumers. With all that in mind, he and I designed his trademark and copyright-protected Pinnacle Club program for real estate agents. In very abbreviated, simplified form, here's how it works:

Via a sequence of direct-mail letters, selected Realtors are invited to accept a free membership in the club. No purchase, no business required, no obligation involved. It may or may not surprise you, but it takes some real selling to get the right agents to accept the free membership, and it required consider-able experimentation on our part to get that step working effectively.

Those who join, free, begin receiving a plethora of benefits they are accustomed to paying for from other sources, including monthly newsletters, monthly audiotapes, e-mail, and fax sales tips, useful information at a members-only Web site, and more every month. On top of that, members get an annual goal-setting package, occasional free admissions to seminars, and other good-ies. With all this material, they also get continuous promotion about Tracy, such as testimonials from the agents who do refer to him, case histories of deals, and other "proof of excellence."

The ideas behind this are simple, let's look at what they aim to accomplish.

GOOD GUILT
First, pile up "good guilt" and a psychic obligation on the agent's/member's part that must be discharged. By burying members in a steady barrage of gifts and valuable information, debt is created. Ethical, honorable people have an imbedded subconscious mech-anism that mandates reciprocity. Some respond quickly; others have gone as long as two years before caving in and referring the first client. Ultimately, well over 50% "convert" to good, frequent, consistent providers of deals.

CREATE DIFFERENTIATION
Mortgages are somewhat commoditized, and real estate agents are barraged by mortgage lenders asking for their business—but most offer the same products and service. This approach is radi-cally, strikingly different.

DEMONSTRATE EXCEPTIONAL EXPERTISE

This approach shows experience not just in handling mortgages without fail but also in helping agents make more money—thus delivering added value.

UTILIZE THE "FEEL" OF MEMBERSHIP

This feeling is a means of attracting business. Members tend to patronize the businesses they are members of more often than they would otherwise.

This system has brought the percentage of Tracy's business coming from real estate agent members up to 72%, eliminated any need to do manual labor prospecting or costly advertising whatsoever, and gradually become known enough via word-of-mouth that agents are seeking Tracy out asking to be let into the club.

This is an approach that might be copied in any number of other selling environments. Admittedly, it requires quite a bit of set-up work, some patient investment, and the discipline to fulfill the monthly program, but it is well worth it.

In the mortgage industry, Tracy's licensees have most of this done for them, and if you happen to be in the mortgage industry, you might want to contact him directly for information, at his web site: www.tracytolleson.com.

CHAPTER 13

Strategy 13
The Magic
of Mystique

P art of the value of what someone does lies in how difficult others think it is to do. For example, in America, people say public speaking is their number one fear. Incredibly, more people are afraid of speaking in public than of getting cancer, having a prolonged illness, or even dying! To me, however, public speaking has become just about the easiest thing I know how to do. I know, though, that I command a significant amount of respect from most groups before I even speak a word, just by virtue of doing what they feel is so terrifyingly difficult to do. It is much, much harder to speak to a group of other professional speakers—because to them, there is no mystique in the speaking.

People wouldn't pay to see a magician perform if they knew exactly how the magic tricks were done. Remove the mystique, and there's no product left. And that's true of most things. In sales and marketing, it's important to create and preserve some mystique, glamour, intrigue, and uniqueness.

Perception Is Reality: The "Story" Is the "Secret Ingredient"

McDonald's special sauce. The formula for Coca-Cola. Colonel Sander's secret recipe. These things preserve some mystique in otherwise mundane products.

Nowhere is this more visibly at work than in the cosmetics and skin-care products field, where I've done a lot of work as an advertising copywriter with infomercials, for private label products and retail salons. If you haven't paid much attention to this business, the next time you're at a department store, stroll slowly past the cosmetic counters. You will be astounded at how many different brand names, colors, scents, and mystifying products there are. The ingredients are incredible: dew collected only from tulips growing on the sunny side of the Swiss Alps, even sheep sperm!

Yet, as much as the consumers hate hearing this, all of these products are pretty much the same. In fact, there's only one manufacturer for every 50 to 100 different brands, labels, and product lines—all with the same ingredients. The only significant differences are the packaging, the price, and the "story."

If you took away the mystique created by the stories, the celebrities, and the advertising, you'd have one generic line of cosmetics, warranting prices 50% to 500% less than today's going rates. But nobody would buy it, and everybody would hate you for telling how the magician did the trick.

Creating Your Own Mystique

Developing mystique is possible for anyone. One technique is what I call "Takeaway Selling," which is explored in detail in Part 5 of this book. Learning to use Takeaway Selling has had greater impact on my personal earnings than any other single thing I've ever discovered or learned, so be sure to study that section of the book. You'll find challenges to some of the ideas regarded as "gospel" about sales success.

Another "trick" is to create your own mystique terminology for what you do, just as the cosmetic manufacturers do. In our self-improvement industry, the once hugely successful and famous EST program built mystique around its unique language and terminology. In EST, you only knew if you had "it" when you got "it," and otherwise you couldn't understand what "it" was. EST's Werner Erhard learned this mystique-creating tactic from his earlier experiences in Mind Dynamics, the human potential seminar arm of the controversial cosmetic sales/pyramid marketing company, Holiday Magic. At introductory seminars for such programs, those already "in" would be talking enthusiastically and happily with one another in a language largely incomprehensible to the new guests. Because outsiders are naturally motivated to become insiders, this situation alone helped sell these programs.

One of the things I've learned in marketing a wide and diverse variety of products and services is that "I've got a secret" is one of the most powerful of all positioning statements. People at all levels, CEO to broom-pusher, desperately want to believe in secrets—that others know some piece of information that has been kept from them that will resolve their biggest problem or fulfill their greatest desire. If you can re-position yourself as a seller of secrets, you'll instantly gain power.

Anyone Can Create Personal Mystique

Certain personal skills that anyone can master if they are made a priority carry mystique values. Salespeople with phenomenal memory skills, for example, have a competitive edge.

I have shared the platform with several different memory trainers over the years, and in every case, audiences are fascinated, impressed, and motivated by the demonstrations of phenomenal memory skills. Harry Lorayne, arguably America's foremost memory expert, can stand at the entrance to an auditorium, meet 100 people—even 200—for the first time and, hours later, go from one to another and correctly call them by name. These people have shown me their "processes," and, although I have not taken the time to do it, I am convinced anybody can learn and master these skills. You can use these skills to remember names and faces, complex technical or financial data, and details of presentations without notes. Something like this could be your path to personal mystique.

I encourage my clients to create proprietary terms, names, and language for what they do whenever possible. My client and Gold/VIP Inner Circle Member, Dr. Charles Martin, a top cosmetic dentist in Virginia, provides "Martin Method Dentistry." Joe Polish's carpet cleaners do "diagnostic carpet audits" when they first visit a home. Platinum Inner Circle Member Ron LeGrand, America's #1 authority on "flipping" real estate, calls it "Quick Turn Real Estate." To many of my clients, I deliver a "Magnetic Marketing Matrix."

Modern Technology Can Confer Mystique

You might be able to use "amazing" technology in your selling activities. An insurance salesperson I know has a small, portable computer and fax machine that he carries with him, which he hooks up to the client's phone. As he interviews the client, he enters all the vital statistics (e.g., age, income, retirement savings goal), then transmits it back to another computer at his office. Minutes later, back through his fax machine, arrives a printout of a personalized insurance plan for that client. It has bar graphs, charts, tables, and is very impressive.

Recently, at my M.D.'s office, I was hooked up to a kinesiology computer, although it has a jazzier name. Essentially, the thing measured nutritional deficiencies by meridian points. As each point was touched, a bar graph appeared on the computer screen, and a tone indicated rise or fall in energy flow. Ultimately, the doohickey dictated the changes and additions needed in my supplement program. I frankly cannot repeat to you the explanation of how this thing worked, but I assure you it sounded as scientific as you can imagine, and the machine put on a dramatic performance. And I'm eating about $1,000.00 a month worth of vitamins, minerals, and plant extracts.

Nothing Beats a "Magical" Demonstration

Can your product be used in a particularly "amazing" demonstration?

I once produced a TV infomercial about a portable "engraving system," and to demonstrate how safe and easy it is, potential customers were invited to engrave a design on an egg shell, without breaking the egg. You've certainly seen the Oreck vacuum cleaner-lifts-a-bowling-ball demo. If you've gone to your county or state fair, you've seen the fellow hawking the "miracle cloth" that sucks up a gallon of spilled cola.

Even products that don't lend themselves to active physical demonstration can still be demo'd. My friend Jeff Paul sold millions of dollars of his financial organizer kit on the home shopping TV network, QVC. The product itself doesn't do anything. It doesn't slice or dice. It's basically a box full of file folders. So the demo Jeff brilliantly devised was a before-and-after, first bringing out a huge pile, a bag full of unsorted bills, credit card statements, etc. and telling everybody this was his wife's filing system "before." Then he showed it all neatly organized, everything easy to find, in one-tenth the space, in his kit, the "after."

This applies to business-to-business (B2B) or industrial selling as well. Years back, I produced a video for a company that sells semi-automated truck tarps to city road maintenance departments. The video featured user testimonials and demonstrations of how quickly, easily, and safely the product worked. I once had a copy machine salesman demo a copier that would not jam by feeding through it a piece of fabric and then a wrinkled wax sandwich wrapper from McDonalds.

How to Unmask and Still Create Mystique

I recommend developing and sustaining some level of mystique in your business, too. If everybody knows everything about your business, you'll often wind up with no business! Yet, sometimes, you can gain by revealing rather than concealing.

A number of years back, I watched Chuck Daly and Brendan Suhr conduct a practice and a coaching session with the Detroit Pistons and then coach a big game. I'm a quick learner, so I think

I understand the structure of what they did and why they did it. But I still couldn't duplicate their experience and talent at applying the process. In fact, I left with a greater appreciation for what they do than I had before.

If what you do creates that kind of awe and respect, then you can create mystique by revealing your process rather than concealing it.

Everything Old Is New Again—At Least It Better Be!

One related matter that messes up a lot of people in marketing is "what's new." A sales rep in one of our companies was once overheard complaining that we hadn't introduced any new products for a long time. "Have all your customers seen all of our products?" I asked. The rep freely admitted they had not. "Then you've got new products," I said.

More than ten years ago, I wrote a book, *The Ultimate Sales Letter* (which is still available in bookstores), in which I reveal and demonstrate each of the 28 steps I follow as a professional, direct-response copywriter to create powerful sales letters or ads for my clients. (My fees start at $15,000.00 and up to as much as $70,000.00 plus royalties.) I revealed every step I take, but still, many people read the book and choose to hire me anyway. Why? Because there's enough intangible creativity in what I do that—even when you know the steps of the process—you may not be able to do it as well as I can. Also, the very fact that I have a systematic, proprietary process influences many clients.

A funny thing occasionally happens in the advertising business: a client will cancel or change an ad campaign that's working perfectly just because they got bored with it and assumed everybody else was, too. That's a bad assumption. There are ad campaigns that sustain success for five, even ten years. These campaigns are old hat to their owners but are new to new customers who are paying attention to them for the first time. If it's unknown to someone, it's a secret—regardless of how routine it may be to you.

I had to learn that in my consulting activities. I charge fees for disclosing knowledge that to me is quite ordinary. To those who need to know it and don't, it's exotic and valuable. For example, I know quite a bit about how to select and obtain mailing lists for just about any purpose. If you need a list of middle-aged dog owners who live in Philadelphia, subscribe to *Better Homes and Gardens*, and have at least one credit card, I know how to get that list. To me, there's nothing to that. To those who don't know and need to, it's worth thousands of dollars.

Don't overlook the importance and value of this lesson. Think carefully about ways you can apply it to your business. John D. Rockefeller said the best route to a fortune is to glamorize the unglamorous. I agree.

CHAPTER 14

Strategy 14
I'd Rather Be Dumb
and Persistent than
Smart and Impatient

A friend of mine tells a story about a dumb frog that fell into a big barrel half full of cream. He was close to drowning, and all the other frogs circled the top of the barrel and laughed and jeered at him. But this frog was so dumb he thought they were cheering him on, so he paddled faster and faster and faster until he churned the cream into butter, and then he was able to hop back out of the barrel.

It's possible to be too smart, to know so much that you know all the reasons why it won't, can't, and shouldn't work. While you are sitting around stymied by all those problems, some dumb frog down the road is doing it!

Now, with all my experience, I have to continually fight the disadvantage of being "too smart." Yes, it can be a disadvantage. You can be too familiar with what has not worked in the past, thus too close-minded to new ideas or re-testing old ones under new conditions.

How Being a Dumb Frog Got this Rookie a Veteran's Top Income—Fast

I remember at the very beginning of my speaking career getting cornered at a National Speakers Association workshop by a very successful, very prominent "old pro." He generously explained to me, at great length, and in great detail, all "the dues" I would have to pay to "get good" before I could even hope to do well in the business. He painted a rather dreary picture of years of begging for low-paid or even zero-compensation opportunities to speak and gain exposure. He told me that if I made a practice of hanging around guys like him and watching their every move, I might amount to something some day.

Finally, when I could get a word in edgewise, I brought up the subject of money. Instead of talking about the number of different audiences he had spoken to or the number of miles he had traveled, I wanted to hear about money: the only real measurement of the worth of a person, product, or service in the marketplace. I asked how much might I expect to earn in the business. His long-winded answer culminated with: "…as much as $100,000.00 a year after 10 or 15 years." I said, "Pardon me, but I made $5,000.00 my first month, and it looks like I'll top $100,000.00 this year, my first year. I was sort of looking for someone who was really doing a big job."

I don't tell that story to be arrogant or to rub the other guy's nose in it, but rather to illustrate this point: this guy did know all the ropes. He really understood the business inside and out and upside down. Compared to him, I was a dumb frog. And I was going about some things the hard way. For example, I was selling myself as a speaker door-to-door, B2B, in person. But through ignorance, confidence, patience, and determination, I was getting spectacular results.

The next time you run into one of these know-it-all "experts" who gives you all the reasons you *can't* succeed, walk away. Who are they—who am I, for that matter—to tell you what *you* can't do? There was a guy pitching in major league baseball with one arm. I wonder how many people tried "for his own good" to convince him to forget about baseball? The experts in the amusement park business laughed Walt Disney out of a meeting room. Among other things, they told him the idea of having just one entrance and exit for a big park was the dumbest idea of the century. I could fill a book with such stories.

Unfortunately, salespeople new to a particular selling environment are often set upon by the grizzled veterans—the resident experts in everything that's already been tried and everything that won't work. Often, their beliefs and biases haven't been tested in years and are erroneous. There's a lot to be said for finding out some things for yourself.

Persistence—Not Stupidity

There's also something to be said—although cautiously—for persistence.

There was a time in my life when I put persistence on a much more exalted pedestal than I do now. In fact, I talked about it in the earlier editions of this book without caveat, which I correct here and now. There is a fine line between essential, admirable persistence and stubborn, costly stupidity. All astute entrepreneurs and marketers learn to welcome the swift sword. To find out what won't work as quickly and cheaply as possible, then on to the next experiment. In concert, though, if they find or figure out something that shows promise, they have bulldog tenacity and tremendous patience in tinkering, tweaking, testing, and tinkering some more to get it fully functional. They are then very resistant to others' discouraging opinions.

Even us legendary experts can be wrong! In my Platinum Inner Circle several years ago, one of its 18 Members, Reed Hoisington, a marketing expert for the mortgage industry, announced a brand new, radical approach he was implementing in selling subscriptions to his publications. I saw and enunciated three major drawbacks to his idea and concluded that it was fraught with more peril than it was worth. The other Members concurred. He ignored us all and tested his premise. Today we all use his strategy.

Does Success—or Failure—Breed Success?

In my speaking career of about 25 years, I've built 11 different platform selling presentations for my own use, culminating with the one I used at all the public seminars with Zig Ziglar and many other engagements from 1993 to 2003. Each one has provided me with excellent incomes. Each one, however, started out as a failure. Each one produced unsatisfactory results the first few times I used it, but each of those times, I learned from the audience reactions what was working and what wasn't. Then I adjusted the presentation, delivered it again, observed and learned, adjusted again, until I finally "hit." Fortunately, each successive one has required less of this, thanks to the cumulative experience. Still, it's the willingness to fail and the failure itself that makes success possible.

My friend Ted Nicholas, famous self-publisher and promoter of the best-selling book *How To Form Your Own Corporation without a Lawyer for Under $75.00*, has sold more than $200 million worth of all of his books through mail-order ads he has written himself. Yet he'll cheerfully tell you that eight out of ten of his ads fail. It's what he learns from these failures that makes it possible for him to create the big winners—direct-response ads that return two, three, four, and even five times their ad cost consistently, month after month, year after year.

Don't ever mistake genius for persistence. When you look at top achievers in any field, selling included, the temptation is to credit them with genius status, which makes it impossible for an ordinary mortal like yourself to match them. But the truth is, more often than not, their current ability to perform is the result of dogged persistence—methodical testing and tinkering, discarding what doesn't work, identifying what does—not gifted genius. And *that* you can replicate.

Resiliency Is Better than Persistence

So much is preached about persistence to salespeople, I want to mention that there is a much more important and useful attitudinal and behavioral skill found in top performers: resiliency. In the Fall/Winter 2002 issue of the Psycho-Cybernetics Foundation's

> # Dan Kennedy's #9
> # No B.S. Truth About Selling
>
> If you're going to arrive at the sales presentation
> that achieves the maximum possible results,
> you're going to have to test a lot of different
> things that flop along the way.

newsletter, I wrote an article titled "Resiliency Is a Skill, Not a Character Trait," which includes six resiliency strategies. You can download it free of charge at www.psycho-cybernetics.com.

CHAPTER 15

Strategy 15
Long Distance Is Nowhere Near as Good as Being There

These days, a lot of companies have cut travel budgets, distance travel is so onerous that I have drastically altered the ways I do business, and e-mail has taken over the world's communication. There are, however, times and circumstances when nothing short of person-to-person, human contact will get the job done, and there are selling situations so lucrative or important that nothing short of that should be employed.

Some years ago, a company I took over was in deep trouble with a primary, essential vendor. The company owed the vendor a huge sum of money, comprising due and past due bills, some as old as 150 days. The vendor had shut off shipments. They would not even ship COD; they wanted payments on the old bills. The comptroller of our company had tried to work some practical arrangement out with the vendor, and several weeks of correspondence and telephone calls had been invested without any results.

I called the vendor and left word for the president that I was flying in to meet with him, would arrive the following morning, and would stay as long as necessary to resolve the problem in a mutually beneficial manner.

I flew to Minneapolis, rented a car, and drove to the vendor's plant. The president and I met for five hours. I let him vent his frustrations; I let him see that I was not equipped with horns, a tail, and a three-pronged pitchfork, and I explained our situation. As the end of the meeting, I had our pending shipments released on an open account, a new open-account credit line sufficient for our needs, and the accumulated amounts due converted to a long-term installment note with no interest. I am absolutely convinced that this could never have been negotiated long distance.

The late Mark McCormack, the famous sports agent with whom I appeared on several seminar programs, said: "I will often fly great distances to meet someone face-to-face, even when I can say much of what needs to be said over the phone." I believe this practice was fundamental to his exceptional success at securing and keeping the top athletes and sports personalities as his clients and for negotiating large numbers of lucrative deals for them. He was willing to do what most people are too lazy and too cheap to do: meet face-to-face.

I have negotiated solutions to huge legal disputes, arranged lines of credit under adverse circumstances, raised capital from private and commercial sources, sold large-fee consulting contracts, and otherwise experienced a lengthy list of notable sales and negotiation victories by doing whatever was necessary to get face-to-face with the other person or people involved. In selling a division of one of my companies to a competitor, I didn't bother with preliminary correspondence or a telephone conversation. I just called the company president and said, "I want to fly over and meet with you for an hour or so to present an idea I think you'll be interested in." By starting out face-to-face, I believe I ensured the success of the proposition and slashed weeks off the time required to create and close the deal.

There is no substitute for face-to-face, personal contact in selling. I *am* a big believer in substituting tools and other marketing methods for person-to-person contact work in prospecting, as I've described elsewhere in this book. I *detest* investing productive personal time in meetings with people who are not qualified or ready to do business. But, on the other hand, I very much prefer getting face-to-face with someone who is qualified and ready to do business. In fact, if the typical sales professionals could switch from spending 80% of their time trying to get to opportunities to sell and only 20% of their time selling to 80% of the time actually selling and only 20% trying to get there, they would increase income four- or five-fold, with no other change in selling skill. And that is why Part 2 of this book may prove to be the single most important set of pages you ever read about your sales career!

Your financial success will be very closely related to your ability to minimize your time spent meeting with people not qualified or ready to buy and to maximize your time spent face-to-face with people who are qualified and ready to buy.

PART 2

How to Stop Prospecting
Once and for All

CHAPTER 16

Positioning, Not Prospecting

I t has been my observation that the weakest link in the selling chain for most salespeople is prospecting. Most people can do at least an adequate job of presenting their products or services, if there's a reasonably interested prospect in front of them. But most of the salespeople I've encountered simply hate prospecting. Consequently, they avoid it, both consciously and unconsciously, and do it only when the dire necessity of imminent starvation pushes them to it. And then they do it poorly.

And do you know what? I hate prospecting too. If I had to acquire my clients, my speaking engagements, my consulting assignments, and my writing projects by prospecting, I'd be driving a cab for a living. To me, prospecting is grubby, unpleasant work. To me, there's no worse way to spend time than talking to people who are not interested, are not qualified to say yes even if they were interested, and who view me as someone they have to defend themselves against.

I'm here to tell you: I do NOT think you should prospect.

What you need to do is to focus on *positioning*. By that I mean positioning yourself so that good, qualified prospects find out about you and seek you out to obtain your expert assistance in solving their problems.

Dan Kennedy's #11 No B.S. Truth About Selling

Prospecting sucks.

Why is this so important? Because when you go to prospects and present yourself, their guard goes up. They perceive you as someone there to get something from them. This is when "sales resistance" sets in. But when somebody discovers you and takes the initiative to seek you out for your expert assistance, then that person's guard is down.

Here are some opportunities for prospects to discover you.

Writing

Writing and being published is a powerful way of helping others discover you. I've written many articles, for free, for all sorts of publications, and I work hard at having books I've written available in bookstores. Why? Because businesspeople read these articles or books, reach the conclusion that I am the expert who can help them, and then seek me out. If I sought them out and put the same information in front of them, as a sales letter or brochure or even by giving them my books, that would not have a tenth of the impact as when they discover the information for themselves.

How does that apply to you? Let's say you're a car salesperson. You can write an article or a regular column for your community newspaper about the inside secrets of buying, trading in, selling, and financing automobiles. You can write about the tax benefits of buying versus leasing and vice versa, what to look for when buying a used car, how to sell your own car, and so on. If you write a whole series of such articles, there may be newspapers, magazines, "shoppers," local union newsletters, and other publications that would be thrilled to publish them.

You could also write a book. Need ideas? How about *Confessions of a Car Salesperson: How to REALLY Get the Best Deal,* or *How To Help Your Teenager Buy and Care for That First Car,* or *Everything Women Should Know Before Buying a Car.* Then you could have that book printed and bound and donate a half-dozen copies to every branch library within 100 miles of where you sell cars. Get local bookstores to take them on consignment. Get a busy local car wash to give them away as gifts to their customers. You could even advertise and sell the book by mail.

Years ago, I consulted with Dr. Robert Kotler, a cosmetic surgeon in Beverly Hills, California, who wrote and published his own book, brilliantly titled *The Consumer's Guide to Cosmetic Surgery.* Thanks to that book and its well-chosen title, he has the credibility of an author. The book gets him invited on local talk shows and invited to lecture. He advertises the book rather than directly advertising his practice, and it is one of the best things he has ever done for his business. I have used "The Consumer's Guide to. . ." or "The Official Guide to. . ." or "The Insider's Guide to. . ." idea in creating hundreds of different comparable selling tools for clients in many different fields.

Barry Kaye, one of the most successful insurance salesmen ever, very effectively uses books he authors in this exact same way. If you read high-end financial publications such as *Worth, Robb Report, Barrons,* or the *Los Angeles Times,* you'll see full-page ads for his books. The books look like "real" books in every way but are actually cleverly disguised sales letters.

In addition to or instead of your own book, you might write for others' publications. If you sell B2B, for example, selling advertising time for a radio station, you could write a series of articles about the basics of radio advertising and then do everything possible to get them published in local business journals, newsletters, newspapers, and magazines.

You could also write and publish a newsletter about the success stories of radio advertising to send out to your clients and selected prospects every month.

Public Speaking

Public speaking is another very effective way to attract favorable attention from people qualified to do business with you. It is also efficient because of the numbers of people reached via each speech.

Open up your local or nearest major city Yellow Pages and look under Associations or Clubs. In one of the cities where I live,

there are more than 2,500 listings in this section of the
phone book. There are business groups, civic groups, and
special interest groups. Most
have monthly meetings. Most
need speakers. Most don't pay
their speakers.

If I'm that car salesperson,
and I have a speech: "Confessions
of a Car Sales-man: How To Get
a REALLY Great Deal," I would
contact—starting with the
A's—the Agri-Business Council,
The American Citizen and

If you want to get really serious about speaking to sell,
whether information products
as I do, or other goods or
services, I have admittedly
expensive but important
resources to recommend to
you, and I invite you to drop
me a personal note requesting
information via fax at 602-
269-3113.

Lawmen Association, the American Legion Posts, the American
Subcontractors, the Association of Realtors, and so on. You get the
idea.

I'd say to these groups: "Listen, I've got a 30-to-45 minute
speech that's fun, funny, and will save your members money the
next time they go to buy a car."

Even though I get paid to speak, as a professional, I say no to
some engagements and yes to others based on how well they position me to be discovered by good, prospective clients. For ten consecutive years, I appeared in 25 to 30 cities a year with Zig Ziglar
on big, public seminars, with up to 35,000 people in attendance. So
why would I travel all the say from Phoenix to Key West, Florida,
on a weekend, to speak to 65 people for a lot less immediate
income than I got from one of these events with Zig? Because most
of those 65 people had paid $7,000.00 EACH to come to a week-long,

intensive seminar to learn how to apply new kinds of direct-marketing methods to their established, existent businesses. They were highly qualified prospects for a number of my professional services. By speaking there, I let them discover me.

Twenty-five years ago, when I was just getting started in public speaking, I had limited financial resources for promotion, but I had a lot of time. I did my own telemarketing and spoke for free at in-office sales meetings, real estate offices, insurance offices, and other businesses. In those speeches, I promoted my own seminars. In one year, I did more than 150 of these little presentations. I improved my presentations with the practice, and I made more than $100,000.00 from promoting my seminars.

Just about anybody could use this same strategy. My Gold/VIP Inner Circle Member Dennis Tubbergen has an entire company devoted to helping financial advisors fill seats at seminars where they can deliver the canned, proven presentations he provides to attract key, targeted clients, such as large-sum IRA account holders. And it is relatively common to see "high-transaction" sales professionals such as investment brokers as well as cosmetic surgeons and cosmetic dentists putting on seminars to attract clients or patients. But I've taught hardware store owners, golf school owners, and home security system salespeople—to name a few—how to effectively sell through seminars.

Publicity

Publicity can change your entire life experience as a sales professional. When somebody writes an article about you and it is published in a newspaper or a magazine, or when you appear as a guest on a radio or TV show, you gain credibility *and* celebrity.

This is, frankly, not an area of expertise for me. Although I have gotten plenty of publicity for my businesses and my books, I'll cheerfully tell you about four people much, much smarter about this than I am. I've had these speak to my Inner Circle Members, and I recommend you seek out and obtain information from them.

One, Raleigh Pinskey, is the author of a terrific book, *101 Ways to Promote Your Business*, available in most bookstores. The second, Paul Hartunian, publishes do-it-yourself kits that make getting local or national publicity a snap. Paul himself actually sold the Brooklyn Bridge (actually pieces of it) entirely via free publicity, has appeared on TV shows ranging from Sally Jesse Raphael and Johnny Carson to CNN news broadcasts, and promoted everything from a *How To Find Your Ideal Mate* book to a charity home for orphaned dogs via newspaper, magazine, radio, and TV—all free. He has been of enormous help to many of my Members. Finally, my Gold/VIP Inner Circle Members, Bill and Stephen Harrison, publish the *Radio/TV Interview Report*, which all TV and radio producers use to find guests to interview. They also host a National Publicity Summit where you can get face to face with about 100 key media contacts all at one time. Look them up at www.freepublicity.com.

I believe any sales pro, selling anything, should make a concerted effort to utilize publicity, to get media exposure, to "get famous" to some degree, because we live in a celebrity- and fame-dominated culture. "Celebrity" is the most powerful marketing force I know of.

Are You Just Another Salesperson?

You might have the solution to a client's greatest need or the answer to his or her most earnest desire, but if you are perceived as "just another salesperson," the client won't pay attention to you. That's what these techniques are all about: positioning yourself in clients' minds as the expert so that they seek you.

By now you may be wondering how to apply some of these ideas to your own business. These ideas are transferable, nearly universal strategies that anyone can use. Suppose, for example, you run a home security systems business.

Easy. Write a book: *Burglars' Seven Secrets for Picking the Houses and Families They Attack.* Write a column for your community newspaper: "Crimestopper Tips." And so on.

You'll find that, just as I said earlier, the writing of a book or a newspaper column will generate business. But you can also use your book to get onto some radio or TV talk shows. Then, watch the news for a new reason why you should appear and be interviewed again, such as a string of unsolved robberies occurring in a neighborhood or the annual release to the media of the crime statistics report.

Next, you could target an appropriate geographic area and start sending a quality newsletter to all the homeowners. Call it "Smart Strategies for Safe Living: How To Safeguard Your Family and Your Home." Provide useful information and tips. Offer your book free.

You could use your book and newsletter to contact and keep contacting reporters, columnists, and editors of every publication in your area as well as talk show hosts and program directors of radio and TV stations. Be polite but persistent. You'll get written about. You'll get publicity. Then you can quote what they say about you. You might wind up with a selling asset like this: *The Cleveland Plain Dealer* said "Robert Bogart knows more about keeping burglars out than the burglars know about getting in!"

That single quote from the Cleveland daily newspaper is a very valuable asset this security system salesman can use and profit from enormously, for years to come.

Another publicity idea for your business would be to exploit your success stories. Suppose shortly after you sell and install a security system in the Browns' home a burglar tries to get in and is scared away by the alarms. When Ms. Brown calls to thank you with this story, grab your camcorder, get out there, and get her testimonial on videotape. With her permission, you might issue a news release to local media, get an article published, then even mail copies to the neighbors.

More ideas: are you licensed and bonded? Have you been in business for 5, 10, 15 years? How many systems have you installed? How many families sleep safely at night and travel on vacation with peace of mind because you've protected their home and possessions? Have you protected any celebrities' homes? Well-known businesspeople in your area? The credibility and/or celebrity of your customer transfers easily to you.

Now, how do you use all this? Well, let me give you one possible scenario—what I would do in this position. When a call comes in from a homeowner asking me about a security system for his home, I would say: "Mr. Homeowner, I'm extremely busy and cannot do justice to your questions today. However, I have a complete information kit that I'll send to you, and I ask that you review it carefully. Then if you think I'm the right expert to assist you with your home security, call me back. If you choose another source, the information will still help you."

Then I would have a messenger deliver a nice, big box to Mr. Homeowner. Inside the box would be my information kit, which would include the following:

- A copy of my book on home security
- An audiocassette of highlights from my best radio talk show interview
- A couple of copies of my newsletter
- A page of quotes, "What the Media Says About Dan Kennedy, Home Security Expert"
- A page that looks like an article about the Browns, head-lined: "Even Though We Thought It Would Never Happen To Us, If We Had Waited Just Three More Days, Our Home Would Have Been Cleaned Out by Burglars!"
- A page titled: "All Sources of Security Assistance Are NOT Equal," which lists your "credibility items" and statistics.
- A list of famous clients and client testimonials.
- Finally, and this is very important, I would include a cer-tificate waiving my usual $250.00 fee for a home and fam-ily protection consultation.

Now, when Mr. Homeowner calls me, what will the position-ing be like? Will he perceive me as "just another salesperson?" Not likely.

The Final Component

Pain and the desire to get relief from pain—physical pain, emotional pain, or financial pain—is the strongest motivational power of all. From the top-of-the-tower corporate boardroom to the working person's small apartment, people are most moved to stop pain.

I want two things when I'm selling. First, I want someone who knows he or she has a problem that is causing some pain and, second, I want someone who perceives me as the person best qualified and most likely to solve that problem and end that pain.

In the example above of the home security business, I first want the prospective client to call me because he or she feels a need for protection. Then, I want to use "tools," not my time and energy, to let the client arrive at the conclusion that I'm the person best qualified to help take care of that need.

"Gee, This Sounds Like a Lot of Work"

Well, I guess it is a lot of work. But when you compare it to all the work inherent in old-fashioned, traditional prospecting, you'll see that my methods provide a better, continuing payoff for effort invested. With my methods, the work is front loaded—you have to do a lot of work to assemble your tools, engineer your system, and get it functional, up, and running. But then it does a lot of work for you. If you stick to the old ways, you have to do a lot of work, the same work, work that inevitably becomes mind-numbing, energy-sapping drudgery over and over and over again, day after excruciating day.

Salespeople dependent on traditional prospecting have to go to sleep most nights wondering where their next prospect is coming from. They get up most mornings without anybody waiting for them to sell to. These salespeople spend a lot of time hanging around the office, at the coffee shop counter, and—in the afternoons—at the movie theater, avoiding prospecting. Then they spend a lot of time doing manual labor prospecting. Ultimately, they spend comparatively little time selling.

The sales professional who masters my methods goes to sleep most nights booked solid for the next day with appointments, with people very likely to buy from him or her.

This is more than a choice of business strategies. This is a lifestyle choice.

CHAPTER 17

How To Use
"Lead Generation Advertising"
to Attract Highly Qualified
Prospects

For more than 20 years, I have been teaching a very specific method for sales professionals of every stripe to end cold prospecting altogether and only go where invited, only call those who've called them first. This method has been adopted, taught, and reproduced in more than 80 different sales niches by my students-turned-master-practitioners-turned-teachers-themselves. Here, I will name only a few, just to give you the idea of the universal applicability of what we'll look at in this chapter.

Real Estate Agents

In this field, I have two different coaches and advisors I've assisted in developing their businesses. One, Craig Proctor, runs giant conferences with 1,000 to 1,500 agents attending and maintains more than 1,000 in his ongoing coaching programs, with most participants investing about $10,000.00 per year to participate. His complete Quantum Leap System includes what we'll cover here.

Significantly, Craig Proctor is the only marketing and sales coach to real estate agents currently excelling as an agent himself; for many years he has ranked in the top ten RE/MAX agents worldwide, and he generates millions of dollars a year in commissions.

Another expert, Craig Forte, publishes "Service for Life," the leading client newsletter used by agents nationwide. This monthly publication, created and mailed for the agents, is a unique type of lead-generation tool.

Insurance, Financial Services

In this area, I have six different "gurus" I've assisted! Jeff Paul, Dean Cipriano, and Pamela Yellen all assist life insurance agents as well as financial planners and advisors with varied applications of what you'll discover in this chapter. Michael Jans does the same for commercial, property, and casualty agents. Dennis Tubbergen and Michael Walters utilize the same strategies specifically to assist financial planners in promoting seminars.

Service Businesses

I will mention five who have excelled in reaching others in their fields: Joe Polish to carpet cleaners, Chet Rowland to pest control operators, Rory Fatt and Michael Attias to restaurants and catering businesses, Ron Ipach to auto repair shop owners.

Mortgage Brokers and Loan Officers

Reed Hoisington provides training, coaching, and actual lead production services. Tracy Tolleson licenses a system for obtaining referrals from real estate agents, described in Chapter 12 of this book.

Again, I have just named a few, all of whom are listed in this book's Resource Directory should you wish to contact them. Combined, these proponents of my no-prospecting method work directly with well over 25,000 sales professionals every year.

I tell you this to motivate interest and establish trust for what I'm about to show you. It is contrary to the manual labor prospecting norms of virtually all sales fields. And, you should know that, I am philosophically opposed to manual labor.

Never the Pest, Always the Welcome Guest

B2B sales professionals are always worrying about "how to get past the gatekeeper," and I'm often asked to answer that question when I'm speaking to sales groups. I refuse because it's the wrong question. It suggests both artifice and difficulty, and I like neither. Instead, the superior question is:

"How can I get sought after and invited in by the decision-maker? "

Regardless of whether you sell B2B or to consumers, my underlying premise is to engineer a situation where you are sought out, invited in, and welcomed as an expert.

Any sales trainer who is still directing you down the "101 tricks for sneaking past the gatekeeper" path should be studiously IGNORED!

The "Welcome Guest Process" in Brief

The process, presented here in very abbreviated form, is actually quite simple. It begins with Step One: one way or another getting qualified, interested prospects to raise their hands. Step Two is then to send them information that raises their interest levels and "pre-sells" you and the value of the appointment itself. Step Three is not to call them, but only to go and sell to them after they call you and ask you to do so.

Successfully implemented and religiously adhered to, this changes the entire life of the sales pro. It multiplies income because your time is not wasted, your energy not wasted, stress is replaced with pleasure, closing rates skyrocket, transaction size increases, and referrals are easier to obtain.

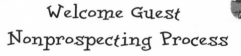

Welcome Guest Nonprospecting Process

1. Get qualified prospect to ask for information from you.

2. Send information that sells you and sells the appointment.

3. Wait—follow-up if you wish by mail but wait until he calls you.

4. Go in as welcome guest (NOT annoying pest).

To begin, then, Step One is called "lead generation." Through an ad, a letter, a postcard, or other means, a qualified lead is produced.

How a Lead Generation Ad Works
Like a "Personals" Ad

If you've ever read, written, or responded to a "personals" ad, you know that they are written to do two things: attract responses from carefully described people and discourage responses from those who do not meet the desired qualifications. The ad might run something like this:

SINGLE WHITE FEMALE seeks single or divorced man, 35 to 49, confident, established in his career, who enjoys travel, theater, cooking, cuddling. No smokers or heavy drinkers, please.

This same approach works for most products or services. You can target your prospect with a lead generation ad. For example, a financial planner might place the following ad:

WARNING FOR MARRIED OWNERS OF BUSINESSES, EXECU-TIVES, AND ENTREPRENEURS WITH TAXABLE INCOMES OVER $150,000.00 PER YEAR: YOU are the government's #1 target. Your net, combined tax load could as much as DOUBLE in the next 12 months. Your pension fund or retirement savings is at new risk. Do you know the TRUTH about the government's plans for your hard-earned money? **MY FREE REPORT: "FINANCIAL**

ALERT!" reveals the details in plain English (NOT financial gob-
bledygook) and provides important strategies and tips. If you earn
over $150,000.00, own a business, own your own home, and have
a pension or retirement savings plan, this report is for you. CALL:
000-000-0000.

Clearly this ad "telegraphs" to certain people and excludes
many others, just like a personals ad.

The person who responds to this ad tells the planner several
very important things. He is married, owns or runs a business,
earns more than $150,000.00 a year, owns (or is buying) a home,
is saving for retirement, is concerned about taxes, is no fan of the
current government administration, and is anxious about his
finances.

Given all this knowledge about this prospect, the financial
planner can create a free report that directly "hits" this person
right where he feels it most. The planner then sends the report
with the package of promotional materials (See Chapter 17,
where such a package is described in the example of the security
system salesperson).

When the phone rings—and it will—you can be sure that this
financial planner is already well-positioned. The prospective
client won't be looking at "just another salesperson"—he will be
seeking out this planner as the expert most likely to solve personal
financial concerns.

Where Do You Run Lead Generation Advertising?

If you sell products or services to businesses, you may use local
area business journals and legal newspapers, the business section

of your city's daily newspaper, or the trade magazines that serve your clients' type of business. As you probably know, there are national or international trade magazines for virtually every type of business and industry, from aluminum manufacturing to zebra breeding. Also, just about every business has at least one association that publishes and usually offers advertising in a newsletter that goes to its members.

If you need help finding the most appropriate publications to advertise in, visit your public library and consult directories such as *Periodicals in Print* and *Encyclopedia of Associations.*

If you sell products to the general public, you might use your city's daily newspaper, weekly community newspapers, local "shoppers," broadcast media (radio or TV), or coupon packs delivered to residences, like Money Mailer or ValPak.

The Postcard Technique

Many salespeople get great results putting their lead generation ad onto a simple postcard and mailing it to lists of likely prospects. The postcard is just about the simplest, least costly advertising vehicle you can find when you consider the cost of a postage stamp.

If you sell to consumers, all sorts of mailing lists are readily available to you from the very simple, such as all the homeowners in a particular postal region, to something quite complicated, such as a "merge-purged" list of subscribers to home decorating magazines who have credit cards, own the homes they live in, fall into certain age and income ranges, and live in particular postal regions.

Lists are also available for business buyers including subscribers to certain trade magazines or other publications, compiled

In most cities, you'll find List Brokers as a heading in the Yellow Pages; one of these local brokers can probably handle needs for simple, local list. If you're interested in something more sophisticated, it will pay you to learn a bit about all the lists and list-related services available.

Go to the nearest main city public library and ask the business librarian for Standard Rate And Data Service (SRDS). Or if you are willing to invest several hundred dollars a year for access, you can go online to www.srds.com. Spending an hour or so going through SRDS will open your eyes to a whole world of opportunity! Basically, if you can describe ideal prospects, you can find available lists to match. And, generally, money spent in list selection is money well spent.

lists of business owners or executives by size of business, type of business, annual sales, number of employees, and other criteria.

Lead Generation Online

These days, a lot of businesses are successfully generating good quantities of quality leads online. The leading chain of fertility clinics gets two million visitors to its Web sites each year, generating tens of thousands of leads. Real estate agents using Craig Proctor's systems generate hundreds of thousands of leads via their Web sites.

Here is a secret to keep in mind: the highest productivity comes from treating the Web site or sites, purchased traffic, and everything done online only as another lead generation medium. Follow up offline, via paper and ink direct mail—not e-mail.

Headlines Are Important

Here's a simple "copy secret" for making these ads, letters, Web sites, and postcards work: The headline is the single most important part of the postcard. For example:

Congratulations!
You've Already Won!

Then you continue:

You've been selected to receive a
fascinating **FREE REPORT** about
(insert your title).

Then you drop in the rest of your lead generation ad's message. Here's a complete example.

Congratulations!
You've Already Won!

You've been selected to receive a copy of
automotive expert Bill Gizmo's informative book,
How To Keep Your Car Alive and Kicking at Minimum Cost,
Without Ever Getting Burnt by Repair Rip-Offs,
absolutely **FREE**.

This book is a $9.95 publisher's price value, and it is full of insider
information that can save every member of your family money.

After all, your family's car(s) represents one of the five biggest investments of your entire life.

Shouldn't you know what insiders—mechanics, race car drivers—know about keeping cars 100% healthy at minimum cost?

Your FREE COPY of this book will be sent to you by mail. There is no cost, no obligation; no strings attached. (This is part of a consumer interest test.) To get your free book, just call (000) 000-0000 and leave your name and address on the recording as instructed.

Who Uses Lead Generation Advertising?

In 1987, a visionary marketer named Jim Bostic switched the entire NordicTrack business from traditional distribution channels to lead generation advertising, followed up by direct-mail and telephone marketing. The company went from small to giant

Lead Generation Message Tips

- Don't try to do too much

- Use a compelling headline

- Keep it simple

- Target

- Fish where the people you want to attract swim

---

at a breakneck pace. NordicTrack's ads usually offer a free video to create response.

Many mail-order and catalog companies use this same marketing model, as do other direct marketers of expensive products for the home. Other fitness devices, Tempur-Pedic and "Sleep Number" beds, and water purifiers are all sold this exact same way.

Although they may not be nearly as noticeable, the continent is full of observant, savvy salespeople who have taken note of this model and applied it to their own businesses and careers.

Here are the secrets to making lead generation advertising work for you, too.

Don't Try to Accomplish Too Much

The only job of lead generation is to produce leads. Do not try to "pre-sell" your product or service, build business name recognition, or otherwise achieve multiple objectives. Focus 100% on getting the right people to respond. Simply getting the right people to step forward, raise their hands, and identify themselves to you is enough.

Use a Powerful, Attention-Grabbing Headline

I've given you a couple of effective examples here. You can come up with others on your own but remember that the headline must be clear, bold, and simple. It must telegraph the promise of a great benefit. And it's very hard to beat "free" as a component part of what you are offering.

Keep It Simple

There's no need to complicate this at all. Focus on a straightforward offer such as a free report, booklet, book, or tape, all of which work very well. Sometimes a free consultation of some kind will work.

TARGET!

Write your message to exclude many and attract the relatively few who are perfectly matched with what you have to offer.

Warning! This Is Not "The Free Road Atlas"

The life insurance industry is famous for truly horrid sales letters seeking appointments with the irrelevant bribe of a free road atlas. That is NOT what I'm talking about here. I advise developing a long sales letter that educates and reinforces the need for the solutions you offer, invalidates other options, pre-sells you as expert and sells the value of the appointment, presented as a "free report" and/or book, audiotape, CD, or videotape. It is relevant to the targeted individual. It is a presales presentation. It is usually designed to screen out and drive off poorly qualified prospects and motivate the best qualified prospects. Ultimately it extends an offer—such as a complementary consultation—with a deadline.

This free report that I am advising you to develop is the equivalent of a sales letter. The techniques for writing such letters are fully described in another book of mine, *The Ultimate Sales Letter* (published by Adams Media and available in bookstores).

ADVERTISE IN MEDIA READ BY THE PEOPLE YOU ARE TRYING TO FLUSH OUT

You may need to test different media before finding one or two that are consistently productive for you. The necessary experimentation is worthwhile, however, because once you get a lead generation system working for you, it can have a very long life.

How to Use Lead Generation to Force Prospects to Give You Information and Grant You Control of the Sales Process

My Gold Inner Circle Member Perry Marshall is a marketing and sales consultant for technology and industrial companies, marketing B2B, and he specializes in online lead generation. He sent me results from a "split-test" conducted for a manufacturer selling to engineers. If you aren't familiar with the idea of split-testing, it means changing only one variable in an ad, letter, Web site, phone script, etc., and trying version Number 1 on half the leads and version Number 2 on the other. On the Internet it's easy to do, as alternating site visitors can be automatically split up and sent to different versions of the same landing page or complete site without them knowing it.

Anyway, one version of this company's site provided

> Actual examples of both of Marshall's Web sites, incidentally, appeared in an issue of my *No B.S. Marketing Letter*, and each issue typically includes several actual examples of ads, letters, sites or other media, illustrating what's working and what isn't. A very good reason to subscribe. Hint. Hint.

a typical brochure online, featuring a Q&A presentation of the company's capabilities and technology applications. Perry's radically different version offered only a "tease" page with a barrier to entry to more information. This page offered basically the same information repositioned as special reports for the engineers but required site visitors to provide complete contact information and answers to a few key questions before they could get to the special reports.

You might think this would suppress response, and in many instances you'd be right, although that might not be a bad thing. I have more to say about deliberately disqualifying prospects later in this book. But in this case, the opposite occurred. The traditional site was converting only 3.5% of the visitors to prospects requesting more information and/or appointments. The new site converted 36.9% of the visitors to real leads. And the ultimate conversions to sales were also higher with the second group than the first.

Anyway, what Perry did for his client was significant yet simple. He repositioned information about their technology applications from brochure fodder to valuable case study information the engineers wanted, then put it out of their reach unless and until they qualified themselves as legitimate prospects and gave permission for follow-up. He erected a barrier to keep the illegitimate prospects out altogether. To do so, he changed from an information dispensing Web site to a pure lead generation Web site.

The Last but First Thing You Need to Know About Lead Generation

It requires the right bait to attract the right critter. If you want a backyard full of deer, do not put a big, 500-pound block of cheddar cheese out there. Your backyard will soon be overrun with rats and mice. If you want deer, try a salt block. However if you want rodents, nix the salt, use the cheese. You can attract any critter to your backyard with the right bait. Similarly, you can get anyone you desire to respond to lead generation advertising, direct mail, and other media—Fortune 500 CEOs, surgeons, stay-at-home moms—if you get the bait right. If you fail, you're using the wrong bait.

PART 3

A No B.S. Start-to-Finish
Structure for the Sale

CHAPTER 18

The Six Steps
of the No
B.S. Sales Process

B efore I had turned 45, I received by mail my invitation to
join AARP, the American Association of Retired Persons.
It was a beautiful direct-mail package, including a personalized letter, a temporary membership card embossed with
my name, and a great premium offer. Only one problem: you had
to be 55 to join. It arrived at my place more than a few years too
soon. And no matter how great the offer was, I wasn't buying.

Many salespeople waste tons of time trying to sell to people
who cannot or will not buy. It's not always as clear-cut as in my
case with AARP, but it still happens often, for a lot of reasons.
Some salespeople are too lazy, too ignorant, or too "chicken" to
properly qualify prospects. I know salespeople in B2B situations,

for example, who know they need to be dealing with the CEO but insist on selling to the personnel directors, training directors, and sales managers instead. Why? It's easier to get to those people. It takes less confidence and self-esteem to deal with those people. The problem is that dealing with those people is ineffective.

Who is the right prospect? The right prospect is

- someone who has a reason for interest in your proposition;
- someone with the financial ability to say yes;
- someone with the authority to say yes;
- someone who is predisposed to say yes.

Interest

Let me explain those four qualifications. First, the prospect has to have a logical reason for interest. Someone who lives in the middle of the Mojave Desert is probably a poor prospect for a yacht. A 92-year-old is a poor prospect for life insurance. Those are obvious. The real-life situations you deal with won't be so obvious.

I don't want to encourage you to prejudge prospects to the extreme. However, you need to determine some sensible link between the prospect and the proposition. If you sell furniture, for example, "homeowner" might be the only link needed. If you sell very high-end, expensive furniture, it might be homeowners only in certain zip codes, with a certain size home, with a certain amount of equity in their homes.

Ability

You need someone with the financial ability to say yes. If you sell to businesses, you might want to zero in on companies that have reported growth in the previous quarter (which is a reflection of their financial strength). If you sell swimming pools, aluminum siding, insurance, remodeling, etc., to homeowners, and are going to do a pre-approach-letter campaign, you might want to have the mailing list of residents in a given area merged with a list of bank credit card holders. The odds are much better that credit card holders are financially able to buy.

Authority

You need to talk to someone with the authority to buy. In consumer selling, that often means that both husband and wife have to be present at the meeting. In B2B marketing, you have to determine who has the authority to spend how much for what. It is easy to ignore this caveat and be a very busy salesperson who is not very busy selling. In my own selling, I'm usually dealing directly with an entrepreneur who has sought me out—with THE decision maker.

Predisposition

I urge salespeople to concentrate on selling to people predisposed to say yes. In mail order, for example, we're much better off marketing to known mail order buyers who also fit our other selection criteria than to people who perfectly fit our selection criteria but have no history of mail-order shopping. If I were selling investment or insurance services, I'd rather contact people who already had some insurance or investments than those who did not. If I sold Lincoln Continentals, I would focus on those predisposed to buying big cars: owners of Lincolns, Cadillacs, and Chryslers with cars nearing trade-in age. Beyond that, by using the "positioning, not prospecting" strategies presented earlier in this book, you can be sure you are investing your time only with those predisposed to buying—*from you.*

Here is the most important thing: you should create your own Highest Probability Prospect Profile, then do everything

No B.S. Sales Process

1. Get *permission* to sell

2. Design an *offer*

3. Deliver a structured *presentation*

4. Use *"emotional logic"*

5. *Close* the sale

you can to invest your money and time in reaching only those people.

Step One: Permission to Sell

The first step in the selling process can be best defined as *obtaining the prospect's permission to sell*. You cannot sell effectively to someone who is mentally or physically backing away from you. Nor can you successfully force someone to pay attention. A person has to choose to be sold to before you can sell to them.

The best advice for securing permission to sell is a question structured like this:

If I could show you how to _____ would you be interested in knowing more about it?

Or, if you prefer to be bolder in your assumption, try this:

> *If I could show you how to _____ you'd be*
> *interested in knowing more about it, wouldn't you?*

The prospect who responds positively to this question gives you permission to sell, and you will have actually built a little box around the person, with his or her cooperation, that virtually guarantees subsequently closing the sale. Now all you have to do is fulfill the "if I could show you how to" conditions, point out that you have done so, say "Eureka!" and ask your prospect to "initial right here."

Here is an actual example I scripted for a client of mine in the investment real estate business. When his reps use it, it works like magic! It is a series of questions.

- Did you pay federal income tax last year?
- Would you be interested in legally reducing the amount of taxes you pay, providing it didn't cost you anything to do so?
- Could you use $5,000.00 to $15,000.00 in extra cash income per year?
- Do you consider yourself an open-minded, positive-thinking person?
- Then, if I could show you how to legally reduce your taxes at no cost to you, increase your income, and associate with others doing the same thing, would you be interested in knowing more?

This series of questions will get the needed permission to sell more than 50% of the time. It can be used in person-to-person prospecting, telemarketing, and, preferably, in lead generation advertising or direct-mail.

I have a "bonus," advanced strategy for you, that secures permission to sell and ensures heightened interest from the prospect. A financial advisor in Chicago who uses it exactly as I scripted targets only multimillionaire business owners and gets invited to meet with 92% of people he approaches. It is that powerful. I call it: guarantee the appointment. Or, buy the appointment. Here's what it reads or sounds like.

> Give me ___ minutes. If I fail to show you at least X# _____ you did not know about and would otherwise not have known about—and that your _____ had not told you about—and you honestly feel I wasted your time, just say the word, and I will pay you $____ as my penalty, right on the spot, cash, on your desk.

Actual example of this template filled in:

> Give me 19 minutes. If I fail to show you three strategies for improving response to your existent advertising or extracting more value from your leads—that your ad agency has not told you about—and you honestly feel I wasted your time, I will pay you $500.00....

That's the one I used in 1974 and 1975 when I first started an advertising consulting business.

Today, I use a very different approach, and to be fair, I should let you see the flip side. These days, I never meet with anyone free, and any new client relationship begins a certain prescribed way. My current approach follows.

> All new client relationships begin with a day of diagnostic and prescriptive consulting, at my base rate, $7,800.00 when you come to me or $8,300.00 plus first class airfare if I come to you, which is rarely possible. At the end of the day, one of three things happens: one,

we've had a good, productive day and you leave happy with strategies to act on.

Two, there's a project or projects you want to hire me to do for you, in which case the initial day's fee is fully credited to the larger project fees and royalties. Or three, you feel your day was unproductive, in which case I gladly refund your fee.

As you can see, I am still guaranteeing the appointment.

Step Two: The Offer

I believe in prefabricating an easy-to-explain, clear, simple, and understandable offer that includes no more than three and preferably only two options.

A two-option offer, commonly called "an either/or" or "an A/B split" usually divides along price lines. You might have a basic, no-frills package at $X, or an options-added, deluxe package at a higher $Y.

Incidentally, my Gold/VIP Member Dr. Charles Martin, a top cosmetic dentist, often presents treatment plans ranging from $30,000.00 to $70,000.00 and typically offers an A or B option. Years ago, I consulted with a company building and selling semi-custom, prefabricated vacation homes. They were "cafeteria selling" from a long, long list of options and attaining an average sale price of $72,000.00 and change. I switched them to an A/B/C option; a basic home, a "Gold" options package, and a "Gold Deluxe" options package. The average sale went from $72,000.00 to $88,000.00. On their 200 sales a year, that added $3.2 million.

Another similar approach is to present the deluxe offer but have a lower cost offer in reserve for a step-down sale.

I'm also a big proponent and user of what I call "the Ginzu knife method" of creating the offer; that is, you offer the main product or service and then add on other benefits. For example, when I offer the cassette learning systems I've been selling so successfully from the platform for the past ten years—more than a million dollars' worth each year—I use an A/B split offer. Package A is the basic transfer of my "marketing mind" to yours via the convenience of 18 audiocassettes. I quickly go through the titles of the cassettes, then I show that the regular catalog price is $139.00, but at the seminar it's discounted to just $99.00. Then I use the "Ginzu knife method" by adding a critique certificate worth $100.00, a copy of one of my books worth another $10.00 retail, and a newsletter.

Package B is the same but includes six more cassettes and my direct marketing action kit, which provides complete, ready-to-use sales letter campaigns, ads, and all other marketing documents for five different types of businesses. I show that this kit alone is catalog-priced at $299.00, so it and Package A together have a value of 438.00, plus the bonuses with Package A bring it up to $548.00. But for the seminar, I offer everything for just $278.00. Then I again use the "Ginzu knife method," offering a consultation certificate and a double guarantee.

The offer is simply summarized as A for $99.00, or B for $278.00. It may interest you that I sell at least twice as many B's as A's.

Step Three: The Presentation

There are several "classic" formulas for the structure of a sales presentation. You can find and learn them in a variety of books, tapes, and articles. They have been tested and proven over time. You do not need any new or more sophisticated formulas. You only need to select the one most appropriate to your particular situation.

One formula you'll hear about is **AIDA: A**ttention, **I**nterest, **D**esire, and **A**ction. First, you get the prospect's attention. This is most commonly done by briefly outlining a set of benefits. Next, you build interest by providing evidence of the benefits with facts, statistics, demonstrations, stories, and testimonials. Then, you create desire by relating the benefits to the prospect. You can also build desire with discounts, incentives, or premiums available for prompt action. Finally, you create action with a closing technique.

Another formula is **PAS: P**roblem, **A**gitate, and **S**olve. This is the formula I prefer to employ whenever possible. I was using it long before I knew what it was called or that it was, in fact, a known formula.

With this formula, you first state a problem and secure the prospect's agreement that the problem exists. For example, you might agree that there is an epidemic of crabgrass in the neighborhood. Next, you get the prospect agitated about the problem, perhaps realizing that crabgrass ruins the appearance of the lawn by damaging the root structure of the healthy grass and that it can damage the lawn mower. Then you produce the solution. Example: Wouldn't it be wonderful if there was a liquid you could spray on your lawn that actually killed crabgrass without damaging the other grass?

This formula is widely used in the advertising of consumer products. The humorous, and memorable, Federal Express commercials do just this.

- The problem: the package didn't arrive.
- Agitation: the employee is in big trouble.
- Solution: "I should have called Federal Express. Why fool around with anybody else?"

I also encourage salespeople to enhance their presentations with visual aides and props. TV has conditioned us to want interesting things to look at. Today, to sell, you almost have to show and tell!

Step Four: Emotional Logic

As far as I know, Zig Ziglar, my speaking colleague of ten years, coined the term "emotional logic in selling." It represents the way people *really* buy: they take buying action spurred on by emotional factors but need logical reasons to justify doing what they really feel like doing.

If you try to get somebody to reason their way to a sale with you, you're going to find tough sledding wherever you go. I don't care if you're selling sophisticated computer systems to Fortune 500 executives, the act of buying will still occur at an emotional level. If you can't create emotional activity and feelings inside your prospect, you won't make many sales.

But you don't want to be an "emotions steamroller" either. If you do, you'll probably wind up buying back as much as you sell or selling to each customer only once and never building valuable relationships. People require reasons to justify their actions. You need to combine emotion with logic.

The last time I bought a new car, the purchase made a lot of sense because my old car was on the verge of requiring some work, and I had no assurance more repair needs weren't going to crop up soon. The same money I was about to spend on repairs could be put into a down payment and, of course, the new car would have a warranty. Also, a new car would be good for my business image and my mental attitude.

Yet, none of those reasons would have motivated me to get the new car if I hadn't *wanted* the new car. You see, a logical argument could be made the other way, too. Even though I needed to put money into repairs for my old car, it was paid off, so there were no payments. Anything less than $500.00 a month in repairs, and I was still ahead of the game in terms of cash flow. The old car looked fine and was perfectly acceptable for my business needs. It was going to take time to shop around and get the new car, and that time, for me, represents an expense.

You have heard the saying, "Find a need and fill it" all your life as a formula for guaranteed wealth. It is more often a formula for guaranteed bankruptcy. Every week some entrepreneur seeks me out with an invention or a product that really does fill an important need but cannot be sold successfully. Why? Because nobody can figure out how to whip up emotional desire for it.

You must merge needs with WANTS. Needs equal logic; wants equal emotion. Most of the time there is a logical argument of comparable strength possible on both sides, for action and against action. And even when there is a legitimate need for the product and a benefit to be gained by having it, that alone cannot tip the scales. The swing factor is emotional.

Use the E-Factors

There are five main Emotional Factors that motivate people to action: love, pride, fear, guilt, and greed. Please note, though, that all are based on a simpler self-interest formula of avoiding pain and obtaining pleasure. For example, let's say you are soliciting money for a nonprofit organization. Some people might feel guilty about how well off they are compared to the world's poor starving children; they might fear bad luck for not doing their share; they might take pride in being able to help; they might be genuinely inspired by love of humankind; or they might see positive public relations benefits for their business by participating. So all five factors might influence them to

Dan Kennedy's E-Factors

1. Fear
2. Guilt
3. Love
4. Pride
5. Greed

participate. But if you go beneath that activity to the very core of response, not giving must be more personally and emotionally painful than giving, and there must be personal and emotional pleasure gained by giving.

The savvy sales pro tries to push all of these buttons in the presentation.

The subject of Emotional Factors is discussed in depth in one of my audiocassette programs, "Midas Touch Selling," available from www.dankennedyproducts.com.

Step Five: Closing the Sale

I once flew across the country seated next to a grizzled direct-sales veteran who had been a door-to-door vacuum cleaner sales-man during the Depression. When hired, he had to study a huge book of answers to 357 different objections and stalls, learn 357 different ways to close a sale, and take a test before getting out into the field where he could make some money. So he learned all 357. And he told me that in his entire sales career since he'd only used three of them.

I believe that closing the sale should be a natural progression not some abrupt jack-in-the-box trick you pull out at the end. If closing is difficult, something is wrong with earlier parts of the selling process. You should not have anxiety or stress about the close because it should happen virtually of its own accord from the momentum you've established. In my own experience, clients will ask: "OK, how do we get started?" before I even have to "close."

Also, if you've asked a series of trial close questions as you've gone along, you will have established the momentum toward the positive closing, and you will have already taken the tension out of asking questions and obtaining answers.

On the other hand, I'm not suggesting you be weak-kneed about closing either. If you aren't fortunate (or good) enough that the prospect jumps ahead of you and literally says, "Let's do it," then you need to accelerate your use of assumptions as you approach the close. Salespeople sell their way right out of sales by using "if" instead of "when" terminology. For example, never say "if you become a member," say "when you become a member," or better "as a member, you get…" If you are meeting the prospect in person, match your words with physical action: "here in your Member Kit, you'll see. . . ."

If you must ask a closing question, there is one simple formula superior to all others. Just about the only closing question structure I bother using or teaching is the simple yes-or-yes question. Would you prefer red or blue? With or without? Today or tomorrow? Pay in three or four installments?

Some people say this is "old hat," and I guess it is. But I haven't found anything better. People usually choose from what's put in front of them. You go into a restaurant, they give you a menu, you choose from the menu. You call up the airline, they tell you what times the flights are, you choose one. So assuming everything else in the sales process has gone well, a two-option, yes-or-yes question is a comfortable way to close the process.

Step Six: The Morning After

Here is a secret few salespeople use—not because it is unknown to them, but because they are too lazy to use it. The secret is to ensure the satisfaction of the customer after the sale. There are several good reasons to build this step into your sales process.

First, some people suffer from "buyer's remorse." They wake up and feel differently about the purchase a day or two after the sale. The emotion of the moment is gone. They are groping for reasons to justify the action.

Buyers like this need "post-sale reassurance." This can often take the form of a well-written letter that thanks a customer for his or her purchase, congratulates him or her on the purchase choice, and restates the reasons why the decision was such a good one. In direct marketing, we call this a "stick letter"—designed to make the sale stick. There's a classic example in my book, *The Ultimate Sales Letter.*

You might also send or deliver a thank-you or welcome gift, a bonus that was never discussed during the sale. Oh, and here's a secret from selling situations where there is typically a high level of buyer's remorse and/or refunds: immediately deliver a "welcome to our customer family" gift of food—cookies, brownies, a big fruit basket, or steaks. This is the close equivalent of "breaking bread" with someone and their office staff or family. It is much harder for someone to cancel a purchase and go back on their commitment after they've eaten your food.

Second, a customer's first purchase should be the beginning of a long, happy, active relationship. You need to do little things after the sale to cement that relationship.

Finally, if you can create a system that motivates your customers or clients to refer others to you, you will never have problems building a giant income and a secure career in selling. Referrals depend on relationships!

PART 4

Dumb and Dumber
Things That Sabotage
Sales Success

CHAPTER 19

B.S. that Sales
Managers Shovel
onto Salespeople

Bluntly, a lot of sales managers aren't parked behind the big desk bellowing at you because they deserve to be there.

Some are sales burnouts, promoted to get them out of the field. Some were top salespeople, now promoted per the Peter Principle to their level of incompetence. Some are woefully lazy. Many are stubborn and close-minded, stuck in whatever era they were at their peak, like the 1950s. Just as the leading cause of death is hospitalization, the prime cause of a lot of sales career death is the sales manager!

Here are the dumbest things I catch such sales managers telling their troops, and my responses.

"The answer to your problem is simple: make more calls."

No, that's not the answer. If you are not being effective at setting appointments, increasing the quantity of ineffective calls only speeds up the pace of failure. If you drink a sip of spoiled milk and feel nauseated, gulping down the rest of the carton isn't the cure.

"Everybody's your prospect."

No, they are not. When everybody's a theoretical prospect, nobody's a real prospect.

"It is easier to sell to someone who isn't interested than it is to find someone who is."

It may be easier to get sex by taking a big club, whacking an unsuspecting woman over the head, dragging her back to your cave and having your way with her than to meet, repeatedly date, get to know, build trust with, and seduce her; but the easier way is an antiquated, primitive—and illegal—approach. Similarly, brute force selling to the uninterested is a primitive, ugly approach. It is also antiquated and is even rapidly becoming illegal; the Do Not Call List, for example, prohibits unwanted telemarketing calls.

"Your problem is you're not motivated."

My entire no-prospecting, "Magnetic Marketing" approach grew out of frustration with motivation. I had the car seat full of motivational tapes, but I still had an empty bank account. The world's greatest attitude is no better than the world's worst attitude if you aren't sitting across from a highly qualified, able-to-buy prospect.

"It's just a numbers game. Keep at it."

OK, there's some truth to this. But—and it's a big but—just stepping up to the plate and taking more swings won't help if you can't hit. It is, in part, a numbers game. But it's also a game of strategy and skill.

How To Tell a Good Sales Manager from a Bad One

Good sales managers teach strategy, coach skills, and work with you to solve problems and manage your opportunities. They do NOT regurgitate any of the above five B.S. clichés. They understand and support sophisticated lead generation and prequalifying efforts to make your time more productive. In fact, they are serious students of marketing and direct marketing, not just sales.

Bad sales managers spit out the above five B.S. clichés so frequently and repeatedly it's as if they have pull-strings in their backs, and computer chips for brains. Saddled with such, you have only two choices: ignore them or get away from them and go and find a better opportunity.

CHAPTER 20

The Six Dumbest Things
Salespeople Do to
Sabotage Themselves

M ost salespeople I know cut their own income by at least 75%, with no help needed from dysfunctional sales managers, corporate home office pinheads, or tough competition. Let's look at the six habits that cost salespeople the most success.

1. Practicing lousy follow-up

If you've ever gone to a trade show as a buyer, as I do, you know that you will get follow-up from almost none of the salespeople you talk to in the booth. You might, might get sent the same dumb brochure you were handed at the booth. That's it.

This pathetic situation actually permeates leads produced from all sources. Most salespeople undervalue leads, have no follow-up system in place, and rarely exhibit any persistence in following up on leads.

Most of the successful clients I work with or who are in my coaching programs have 8 to 28 steps in their prospect follow-up sequences, which may include multiple mailings, e-mail, fax, invitations to lunches, seminars, teleseminars, online "Webinars," and more. For example, a client, a salesman of a $20,000.00 business product, has gone from $200,000.00 to $500,000.00 a year in commissions in the past 24 months. At my urging, he has added five follow-up steps beyond his norm: three lengthy letters two weeks apart followed by a faxed invitation to a group teleseminar held only for these unconverted leads. He closes as many sales from these added five steps as from his regular selling activity.

2. Hanging out with losers

In virtually every sales organization, 5% of the sales staff makes 80% of the money. If you are wasting your time hanging around 95%ers, you get crumbs.

3. Hanging out with the losers at the bar, strip club, or coffee shop

No additional commentary needed.

4. Wasting time

Walk into the typical auto showroom, pool and patio store, or some other business where customers come to the salespeople. Watch everybody. Most of the salespeople are standing around waiting, talking to each other, munching doughnuts, and drinking coffee. Not selling. The two car salesmen I know who each earn over $200,000.00 a year never take a walk-in and never stand around waiting for a turn. They are busy with appointments, which are generated proactively.

Bill Glazer, who publishes my *No B.S. Marketing Letter* and is a marketing coach to retail store owners, also owns two thriving menswear stores in Baltimore. His in-store clothing salespeople do well over 40% of their business in preset appointments with their customers. When they aren't engaged in selling, they are mailing or calling their clients to set up appointments, not standing around sucking up java.

Incidentally, my other book *No B.S. Time Management* is mandatory reading.

5. Not creating systems

The seat-of-the-pants salesperson will never, ever match the income of the systemized salesperson. The top producers live by systems.

They have a system for generating a steady stream of good leads from multiple sources.

They have an intake system for those leads, for categorizing them, managing them, following up on them with multiple steps and multiple types of media. For example, if the system calls for four letters, each seven days apart, then by golly, each prospect gets four letters seven days apart.

Top performers also have a system for selling. My own "million-dollar presentation" I use from the platform and the process and language I use in selling my consulting and copywriting services are all scripted, rehearsed, fine-tuned, and memorized.

$\AA$ lot of my clients and thousands of the
sales professionals my clients work with rely on a
company called Automated Marketing Solutions to
support this type of system. AMS provides toll-free
recorded message lines for lead capture, Web sites
for lead capture, automated e-mail follow-up online,
transcription, and e-mail of leads to the salesperson
for his follow-up, even mailing of "free reports" for
salespeople to their leads. You can contact them at
www.findmeleads.com.

I subscribe to David Sandler's axiom: if you do not have a system
for selling, you are at the mercy of the prospect's system for buying (or not buying).

Finally, top performers have an organized, multistep system
for encouraging, obtaining, and rewarding referrals.

6. Living with poor self-discipline

For several years, I spoke at about 20 programs a year immediately following General Norman Schwarzkopf. Norm echoed
some classic advice to military men and women: the difference
between a live soldier and a dead one is discipline.

Top salespeople hold themselves accountable. They organize
each week's and day's work, they have goals and standards and
benchmarks, they get going early in the morning, and they keep
going all day.

PART 5

My Biggest Secret to
Exceptional Results in Selling:
Takeaway Selling

CHAPTER 21

The Awesome
Power of
Takeaway Selling

I n this chapter of the book, I reveal **THE** secret I have relied on most heavily from 1993 to the present, during which my personal earnings skyrocketed along with my prominence in the fields in which I work.

Proving the Theory of Supply and Demand

In many ways, Takeaway Selling contradicts classic wisdom about selling. One of the most important underlying principles behind Takeaway Selling is the law of supply and demand and how it affects people's desires. As a rule of thumb, the less accessible something is, the greater the value that gets placed on it, and the more people want it.

I spent too many years of my adult life dead broke, and that was a mystery to me for quite a while. I had my dog-eared copy of *Think and Grow Rich*, kept a car seat full of motivational tapes, went to seminars, faced the mirror and said my positive affirmations out loud every morning, tried hypnosis, subliminals, and every other darned thing; and I had some pretty sharp skills. And I was still walking around with a big, blustery smile on my face with nothing but hungry moths in my wallet. Finally, I determined that the missing link to success is mastering supply and demand because as soon as there is a consistently greater demand for your services than there is supply of your time, it's ridiculously easy to be successful.

In my businesses, as a consultant, copywriter, and speaker, I've learned that demand definitely breeds demand. The busier I am, the more people want my services; the less accessible I am, the more I'm appreciated; the less the supply of me, the greater the demand—and the virtual absence of fee resistance. That's one of the reasons I now publish a frequently updated, detailed copy of my schedule. I send it to clients and prospective clients, and when they see the supply-demand ratio, they act.

These days, this technique is 100% legitimate; I really am overbooked, and it is a struggle to fit in new clients, projects, and engagements. But I'll frankly tell you that I did my best to create this appearance and foster this image before it was a total reality. For example, even when I'm in the office, I very, very rarely take an incoming call from anybody but a VIP client, and that's been my policy for years—years before it was a time management necessity. Often, to even have a phone conversation with me, it has to be scheduled as an appointment several days to a week in advance.

I also haven't used business cards in years. At speaking engagements, there are always a few people who do not rush to purchase the materials I offer but instead come to me asking for my business card. I tell them that I don't believe in business cards, and I tell them why: if they aren't interested enough in what I've talked about here to invest a couple of hundred dollars, why would I want them calling me at my office? When new prospects call my office, they're usually advised to send a brief memo to my attention, describing what they wish to discuss with me, so I can them call them at my convenience. Again, these are now time management necessities. But I implemented them for their sales impact before they became unavoidable.

Dan Kennedy's #12
No B.S. Truth About Selling

When have you ever heard of anybody going to see
the wise man at the BOTTOM of the mountain?

A friend of mine sells a high-priced business opportunity. When prospects answer his ad, they are sent an introductory letter and a four-page questionnaire that must be filled out and returned before my friend will send the company's brochure, other literature, and videotape. Then, before my friend will get on the phone and talk with a prospect, he has to complete and send in a second questionnaire and provide three employment or character references. Finally, after their phone conversation, the prospect (called an "applicant" at this point) must get on an airplane, come to the company's headquarters, be interviewed by two different executives, and then, finally, the prospect is allowed to meet my friend and turn in a check and buy the business opportunity.

My Gold/VIP Member Dr. Tom Orent sells a $40,000.00 per year coaching program to dentists. They must fill out and submit a 16-page application before he will talk to them about his program.

One of the highest-fee business consultants in America is famous for the fact that he will not get on an airplane—ever. If you want to meet with him, you have got to go to him, and that's all there is to it. I have gotten very close to that practice now, myself.

How a Starving Dog Trainer Rid Her Finances of Fleas, Once and for All

At a seminar a few years ago, Elizabeth R. cornered me on a break to tell me her troubles. She was a very talented, very capable dog obedience trainer. Her credentials, references, and testimonials were pretty impressive. She had a jazzy brochure. She resided in a high-income area. But she was having a devil of a time making ends meet. "What do you charge?" I asked. "$20.00 an hour," she answered—and she went to the customers' homes to train their dogs.

I told her, "You are a professional—a dog therapist. Triple your fee, make the client bring the dog to you, and do not even agree to accept a new client's dog until the dog takes your special IQ test for dogs. Charge a fee for the initial client consultation and test the dog to be sure it has enough basic intelligence and the proper attitude to respond to training. And make each new client wait at least a week before you fit him or her in.

"Immediately send a letter to all your past clients, thanking them for all their past referrals but advising them that, because of the overwhelming demand, you have no choice but to impose new restrictions on accepting new clients. Send a similar letter to present clients but offer them services at your old fees for six more months. Stop answering your own phone. Dress better."

This kind of move takes guts. When you are sitting there, twiddling your thumbs and worrying about the checkbook balance, it requires a lot of nerve *not* to grab that phone yourself on the first ring, jump in, and sell, sell, sell. I know; I've been there.

A few months after the seminar Elizabeth dropped me a note, letting me know she'd had her first $10,000.00 month and felt certain she'd make more than $100,000.00 in the next year.

A Real Estate Agent to Learn From

Real estate agent Peggy B. gets 70% of her listings from referrals, 30% from advertising. Either way, when someone interested in listing a home with Peggy calls her office, the receptionist transfers the call to one of Peggy's three assistants. The assistant explains that, because Peggy's services are so much in demand, she employs three client service specialists to—among other things—screen her calls and make certain that the caller's property meets the strict criteria Peggy has for her listings. Otherwise, the caller will be referred to another agent.

The assistant then asks the caller a dozen questions, completing a form as she goes. Ultimately, an appointment is set for Peggy to visit the client's home several days later.

Next, a videotape "documentary" about Peggy, her unusual success, and the thorough services she provides, is delivered by messenger to the caller's home. The assistant calls the day of the appointment to be certain that both husband and wife have watched the video. In the rare instance where they have not, the assistant postpones or cancels the appointment.

At the appointment time, the assistant, not Peggy, arrives at the home. She bears a gift of a little package of cookies from a local, upscale bakery, and the bad news that Peggy will be delayed by no more than 20 minutes at a closing. In the meantime, the assistant provides information on the recent selling prices of comparable nearby homes, the length of times they've been on the market, related data, and how that is used to calculate a reasonable range from which Peggy will determine their best listing price. Peggy tells me it's better to have this "dirty work" done by the assistant before she arrives, giving the client time to think about those numbers versus their all-too-often unrealistic expectations concerning the price.

About 15 minutes later, Peggy calls from her car phone to announce her imminent arrival. Minutes later, in one of her bright-colored, gold-trimmed Cadillacs, Peggy arrives.

After apologies and pleasantries, she listens as her assistant quickly "briefs" her, summarizing what's been discussed so far, and setting up the price range. Next, Peggy asks if, while they talk, it's OK if her assistant goes through the house and takes photographs for potential use in advertising, brochures, and displays at the office. (This, in case you don't recognize it, is a trial close. Why would they let her go ahead with photography if they weren't going to list the house with Peggy?)

The assistant takes her top-quality camera and goes about her business, while Peggy uses her "flip book" to explain the ten steps they'll use together to get the best possible price for the home in the shortest possible time. At the end, there's a listing agreement, already partially completed by the assistant from the information obtained over the phone.

Last year, Peggy immediately listed 92% of the homes where she made this listing presentation. In almost every one of those cases, Peggy charged an "advertising cost" to the client and collected that from the new client on the spot, too—something most agents do not do. And, of the 8% she did not get immediately, half came to her later.

"What happens," I asked Peggy, "when the client objects to that charge, or the price you want them to set, or they question whether or not you'll be able to give their property's sale enough attention, considering how busy you are?"

She replied,

> It rarely happens because of the way our relationship is set up from the beginning. But when it does, I TAKE IT AWAY from them. I'll say something like "Well, different approaches are right for different people. You may be more comfortable with a more conventional agent, somebody who will sit here day after day on open houses, be around the office whenever you call, and not be so selective about taking clients." Then I'll pull out my address book and start to recommend a couple of "those kinds" of agents. The client invariably back pedals.

The Power of Disqualification

Most salespeople complain about having too few leads and struggle mightily to get the ones they have. The sales professionals using all my "Magnetic Marketing" methods attract more leads than they can handle. This supports a radical shift in think-ing—to disqualifying prospects as quickly as possible. When you have plenty of choices about who to invest time in, you only want to invest it in what I call highest probability prospects, get-ting rid of the others, fast. Ruthlessly.

Case in point: on the next page is the back side of the busi-ness card used by my long-time client and friend, Joe Polish, president of Piranha Marketing.

It is a direct "knockoff" of copy I used a decade earlier when I still carried business cards. This copy is intended as the "warn-ing" its headline promises: do NOT waste my time!

My Platinum Member John Paul Mendocha is the creator of the SpeedSelling System, which is delivered to salespeople in dozens of different fields via seminars and telecoaching pro-grams. He is today's leading advocate of disqualifying prospects and teaches "Five Power DisQualifiers." John told me this story of one of his earliest experiences in selling that led to his commit-ment to this idea:

> Early in my sales career, I was moved to a new terri-tory, selling for a manufacturer that had done a lot of advertising and generated a giant stack of leads for their newest product—so many the rep already there couldn't handle them all, so reinforcements were dispatched. Me. My colleague, who had been in this territory for years, was busy wearing out his radial tires driving all over southern California following up on all these leads. I quickly determined this was not for me. I spent an entire weekend developing a master list of 150 qualifying ques-tions about this product and the company that would buy it. After much analysis, I found within the 150 just

! Warning !
Five Things You Need to Know
About Joe Polish and Piranha

1. Joe Polish is blunt, straightforward and may NOT tell you what you want to hear.

2. Only those very serious about making money, utilizing unusual and exceptionally effective marketing strategies, and those really ready to change should contact Joe.

3. Joe rarely takes unscheduled calls; however he does have an excellent staff in place. They can be very helpful and you are welcome to call them.

4. In many cases, staff or Joe will recommend books, courses or tools that best address your questions and needs. Individual consultation requires substantial investment; however many situations are well served by the products Joe has developed or obtained.

5. Do not be disappointed or frustrated by Joe's refusal to dispense free advice. Free advice is rarely a bargain for the recipient, nor a fair return on investment and experience for the giver.

three questions the prospect had to answer yes in order for them to use this product. On Monday morning, I started calling the leads and immediately asking them the three questions. If they answered no to any of the three, I moved on to the next lead. The ones who answered yes to all three, I made appointments with, and very successfully and efficiently made sales to—a lot more sales, a lot faster than my colleague.

I have many stories of my own about the power of disqualification, and I totally concur with John: it is the core, essential secret of efficient selling, what he calls SpeedSelling.

A number of years back, through a sequence of unusual circumstances, I wound up majority stockholder in and CEO of a custom manufacturing company in a tiny niche. This company was losing money at a breakneck pace, had every business problem imaginable, and a few unimaginable ones. As the firm had no cash, I was not only CEO but also vice presidents plural of everything, and national sales manager. After about a month as sales manager, I made an astounding discovery: we were manufacturing a lot more quotes than anything else. Our two sales reps were spending half their time doing quotes. We were a quote machine. Unfortunately, only 20% of the clients being provided with quotes were converting, and of those, it was taking an average of five different quotes to wind up with one order. There was a lot of "quote it again with blue boxes instead of four-color" sort of activity.

To the screaming anguish of the sales reps, I instituted a new policy: $500.00 charged to any new, prospective client for quotes on a project, $200.00 to all but a few "Grade AAA" established clients; the fees for quotes would be applied to the order but otherwise were nonrefundable and must be paid in advance by credit card or check. For about two weeks, the reps alternated the death march in and out of my office, weeping, wailing, and gnashing their teeth over all the prospects who were outraged and going elsewhere for quotes. However, at the end of 60 days, the results told a different story. We now issued about one-third fewer new project quotes and had driven off only 18 of about 300 past accounts, and all of those 18 were high in the pain-in-rear quotient, low in profit. Conversions on the two-thirds new project quotes had doubled. The speed of the process, quote to conversion, went from an average of 40 days to 15, thanks to another of my new policies: quote fee refundable only for 21 days. Further, overall sales were up because the reps had more time to sell and to follow up on really viable leads. They had less activity swirling around them and thus got a clearer, more harshly accurate picture of what might close in the immediate future. One of the two, who actually "got it," tripled her commissions over the next three months. By forcing her to disqualify, I multiplied her income.

Being aggressive about disqualifying a prospect takes courage. Being a sales wimp, though, carries its own high price in pain.

A Fundamental Choice

Whether you use Takeaway Selling or not is a fundamental choice about how you are going to go through your career and what kind of experience it is going to be for you and for your customer or clients. Takeaway Selling actually is win-win. Clients feel good about being privileged, being special, being in an elite group, and if they get that feeling by doing business with you, then you are providing significant added value. You will have much more energy and enthusiasm, bring more creativity to your clients' needs, and derive greater satisfaction from your daily experience if you are dealing with people who do feel privileged dealing with you!

PART 6

Sales Tools
and Technology

CHAPTER 22

The Brave
New World
of Tele-Selling

I n the past decade, the sales world has been flooded with new technology. A plethora of software is now available for contact management, time management, automated sending of letters, and so on. There's voice mail, cell phones, fax-on-demand and fax broadcasting, e-mail, Internet Web sites, and laptop or even palm-size computers. As you might imagine, I have some "no b.s." observations about all this. In this chapter, we'll tackle things telephonic, in the next, things hooked to the computer.

"Mr. Watson, Answer the Darned Phone!"

Let's tackle voice mail first. I hate being stuck on the wrong end of this monster, waiting to wade through a menu of choices, pushing "17," and being rerouted to another menu. However, the general public and most businesspeople have become accustomed to using voice mail, and, from the sales professional's standpoint, its virtues outweigh its negatives. It's often even better than having a live receptionist or secretary.

The trick to using voice mail as your message taker is to make it as painless as possible for customers, clients, and prospects. That may mean having one highly publicized number for prospects but another, private number for clients. The voice mail for prospects could have more elaborate and/or different information, screening, and menu options than the number for clients. You do want to manage expectations carefully, though; people leaving voice-mail messages will be impatient if not called back quickly, unless you warn them in advance. If you check messages and return calls frequently all day long, no problem. But if you let an afternoon's messages accumulate until the end of the day and deal with most of them the next morning, your message needs to advise callers of that, to preempt their frustration over your unreturned calls. Also, every sales professional needs a *complete* strategy for dealing with telephone calls, which I discuss in detail in my book *No B.S. Time Management*. The telephone can be a huge "time suck," and you need very specific techniques for managing it.

The sophisticated options available for voice mail are constantly increasing. ATG Technologies, one of the companies I recommend to my Inner Circle Members, offers a hybrid voice-mail service with a live secretarial service called PAT-Live. If you wish, your one number in their service can receive voice mail, e-mail, and faxes; translate the e-mail and faxes into spoken-word messages like the voice mail; or transcribe everything and deliver it to

*O*ne of the things I like to do with other people's voice mail is to "force" telephone appointments. For example, if I have a dozen or so people who've been trying to reach me, I'll set aside a two-hour block late in the day to call them, virtually certain to get their voice mail, and leave a message that I'll be taking calls at a particular number between x-hour and y-hour the next day. Then I'll say something like, "If you can call me between 9 A.M. and 9:30 A.M., that'll be best, but any time between 9 A.M. and 12 noon is fine. If you get a busy signal, please just call back—do NOT leave a message." Then I'll assign the next couple of people the range of 9:30 A.M. to 10 A.M.; the next couple, 10 A.M. to 10:30 A.M.; and so on. In about 80% of the cases, I get the return calls exactly when I've asked for them, and I'm able to efficiently handle a long list of calls without playing voice-mail phone tag. By the way, you can do this work while sitting out by your pool (or a hotel pool if on the road), enjoying sun and fresh air. You can even take these calls on your cell phone while driving from one city to the next.

you wherever you are by e-mail or fax. You can also call in and dictate responses to go out via e-mail, fax, or a call made for you by one of the secretaries. You can trigger certain callers' numbers

Here and now, I'll just make the point that, for too many sales professionals, their own telephones have become enemy rather than ally, and their voice mail has become an impenetrable, frustrating barrier to prospects and clients rather than a helpful tool. This is NOT necessary. You can determine to make the telephone work for you in every way.

to get priority over others and arrange to be tracked down via pager; you can also set up a "find me" process that tries to reach (in the order you request) your office phone, your cell phone, your car phone, your home phone, and your golf cart phone. And you can "re-engineer" all that for your convenience day by day, to coordinate with what you'll be doing and where you'll be that day.

Personally, I use none of this. I refuse to carry a cell phone or use e-mail, and I have rigid procedures for controlling access to me, allowing me to work without interruption or distraction and respond to people in the manner that suits me best. And I believe you can position yourself with clients and prospects so you can dictate these rules of engagement without sacrificing business or damaging relationships. Again, I deal with this in detail in the *No B.S. Time Management* book.

Let the Phone Do Sales Work for You

A variation of regular voice mail is the "recorded message" that dispenses information automatically so you don't have to. This goes beyond message-taking into automated information delivery.

For example, many real estate agents now build a menu into their voice mail so prospects calling for information about currently listed and available properties can press one to hear about west-side properties, two for lake-side, or three for downtown condos. Craig Proctor, mentioned earlier in this book, pioneered and perfected the use of this technology in selling real estate and now teaches other agents an entire marketing system built around it.

Joe Polish teaches carpet cleaners how to drive people to a "consumer awareness message"—a free, recorded message that presells prospective customers very effectively.

The advertised "free recorded message" often boosts response to advertisements, sales letters, brochures, or catalogs and is an effective and efficient prospecting tool for sales pros—just as it is an advertising tool for business owners. For example, my friend and client Rory Fatt, of Restaurant Marketing Systems in Vancouver, Canada, teaches restaurant owners how to use the free recorded message as a means of running smaller, cheaper ads and then dispensing information about the restaurant, cuisine, chef's expertise, specials, events, and opening hours via a recorded message.

The free recorded message is a staple of my "Magnetic Marketing." I try to get every client to use this tool and add it to their ads, mailings, even business cards.

Automated Marketing Solutions is the company most of my clients rely on to provide and operate their recorded message "hotlines," transcribe the leads, and even manage follow-up mailings. Its president, Ron Romano, is the leading expert in using this and other automated information delivery, prospect screening, and lead capture technologies.

Selling Via Conference Calls

More than 100 of my clients and Inner Circle Members routinely and frequently use "tele-seminars" or conference calls to sell, with optimum efficiency. Usually, unconverted and stubbornly

H ere are a few examples of diverse applications of tele-seminars my clients and I have used.

A software company serving the heating/air conditioning industry drives unconverted prospects to a tele-seminar on "Five Ways to Improve HVAC Business Profits with Contact, Customer, Sales, and Operations Management Software."

A weight-loss company drives unconverted prospects to a weekly tele-seminar featuring question-and-answer time with the doctor who developed its products.

An investment company offers a single monthly tele-seminar for people who registered to attend its free introductory seminars in various cities but failed to show up. It has had as many as 1,800 prospects on one call.

Numerous conference call companies can provide the services you need to conduct these calls.

resistant prospects are invited to a free or for-fee 30-, 60-, or 90-minute tele-seminar, with the sales pro hosting. During the call, several successful users of the product will be interviewed, some education will be offered, and sometimes, operator-controlled question-and-answer sessions will be conducted. Hundreds of prospects can be handled on the same call.

Dialing for Dollars, One on One

As I'm writing this, the national Do Not Call List has gone into effect, although not yet locked in rock as law. Basically, though, the days of cold telephone prospecting from real estate agents to FSBOs (For Sale By Owners), mortgage lenders to homeowners, actually anybody trying to get appointments with consumers, is—if not dead—on a respirator. From my perspective, it does not matter because there's nothing more primitive and ignorant than cold telephone prospecting anyway. I have been opposed to this practice for years. I think anyone still teaching or goading sales-people to do this is foolish.

Although legal, I'm equally opposed to B2B cold calling. Cold calling to businesses is very poor positioning, raises problems with gate-keepers, and wastes tons of time. Some sales professionals engage in it more as a place to hide and look busy than as a productive way of selling.

However, following up with people who have asked you for information with a direct, personal phone call is often extremely effective and productive. In fact, there's rarely a marketing and sales situation involving follow-up on leads where this kind of direct calling won't pay off. Most of the clients I work with insert the proactive, one-on-one follow-up call relatively late in a planned sequence of follow-up steps. The preference is still to do things that motivate the prospect to call rather than calling the prospect.

Dialing for Dollars by Robot

Another tele-technology I like a lot, and always look for opportunities to use, is voice broadcast. This is more applicable if selling to consumers than B2B, although it can have B2B applications, especially at the small-business level.

A voice broadcast is a brief message you can record in your own voice that is automatically delivered to 100 or 10,000 numbers simultaneously and simulates or mimics an individually made, personal call. Most of the time, I advise clients to deliver these messages only to voice mail and answering machines; the robot just hangs up if a human answers at the other end. When the recipient comes home and checks his answering machine, he can't tell a voice broadcast message from a person's message. For example, here's the message created by an Inner Circle Member who is in the swimming pool and spa business. He delivers this message to all his unconverted prospects—people who've requested information sent by mail, visited his Web site, or come into his stores but not purchased—each time he will have an exhibit at a home improvement or mall show.

> "Hi, this is Bob (Name Withheld); sorry I missed you. I was calling to personally invite you to drop by our big exhibit at the Home Show this coming weekend and see our six newest pools and spas. You were interested in one of our pools or spas, and I'm sure you'll love one of these new models—and our new 0%, 60-month financing.

There's a free dinner for two certificate waiting for you, just for dropping by."

Bill Glazer—who publishes my *No B.S. Marketing Letter*, consults with retailers, and owns two thriving menswear stores—uses voice broadcasting 10 to 20 times a year for his stores. He also provides proven voice broadcast campaigns to thousands of other stores nationwide.

I have a client who delivers more than 70,000 voice broadcast messages a year to confirm appointments for his salespeople and to remind registrants to attend his company's free seminars. He has replaced a huge room of employees making these calls with automated voice broadcasting, slashed hundreds of thousands of dollars of costs, and improved results.

Automated Marketing Solutions, mentioned earlier, is one of the companies providing voice broadcast services.

Just the Fax, Ma'am

I am in love with the fax machine and all that it can do to facilitate the selling process. (It's my kind of technology: one button.) First, it lets you respond quickly (if not instantaneously, at least without mail delay), easily, and at virtually no cost to requests for information and quotes. Because the fax accurately reproduces what you send (unlike e-mail), you can transmit sales letters with all the embellishments (such as underlining and bold face type) and be assured it will reappear at the other end as intended.

One of the best benefits of communicating by fax is that, in most offices, incoming faxes still get priority over incoming mail. Your fax leaps to the top of the pile. In many businesses, faxes are treated like phone messages in that they are dispensed to or picked up by recipients a number of times each day, instead of being in one fat stack of daily mail.

It's also easier to get past "gatekeepers" to decision makers (if you know their name) with a fax than with mail. The combination of a fax's immediacy and perceived priority, use of a personalized cover sheet, and separation from mail routinely screened and sorted by the gatekeeper often guarantees the fax safe passage to the decision maker's hands.

No other medium combines this kind of favored priority handling with its near-zero cost.

One of the most interesting uses of the fax for prospecting purposes is "broadcast fax." In the past, this tool was very useful in situations where you may have been seeking qualified leads from a large pool of potential prospects. Unfortunately, new laws and civil litigation have, as of this writing, all but eliminated the safe and legal use of broadcast fax for this purpose. However, it is still extremely effective and efficient for permission-based marketing; follow-up with prospects, and frequent communication with clients who have given permission to receive communication from you.

For example, I coached a top salesman of a wide variety of used and reconditioned industrial equipment who more than doubled his income the year he started sending a weekly fax to his top 500 accounts. In those faxes, he keeps clients apprised of the newest pieces of equipment available and shares business tips, equipment maintenance tips, and client testimonials.

My client Dr. Ben Altadonna, who sells training, seminars, and other services to chiropractors, is one of the most consistent, successful users of broadcast fax campaigns to his past customers. His campaigns drive them to join tele-seminars, to visit Web sites, and to request printed information.

This is a tool just about any B2B sales professional can use. On a small scale, you can program numbers into your own fax machine to do your own fax broadcasting. Or you can use a service, such as Automated Marketing Solutions, to simultaneously fax 50, 500, 5,000, or 50,000.

A Legal Notice

Several times in this chapter I've mentioned legal matters; you need to be aware of various federal, state, and—in some cases—local laws governing telemarketing, voice broadcasting, and fax broadcasting. And you need to comply with the laws governing your particular application. Regrettably, by law, I can't practice law and give you legal advice here in this book. Learning about the laws and following them is your responsibility.

CHAPTER 23

The Brave New World of Techno-Selling

Anyone who knows me well knows I personally dislike using a lot of technology. I refuse to use e-mail, and I've never once gone on the Internet to go to a Web site—if I must read one, my assistant or the client downloads it and gives it to me on paper. I've found it hard to make notes, underline, and use a yellow highlighter pen on the computer screen. My legendary Luddite preferences do not, however, interfere with my using technology for marketing and selling when it is appropriate and useful. In fact, I've made hundreds of thousands of dollars from my Web sites and e-mail marketing; and maybe of greater significance, I've been paid huge sums to write sales copy for Web sites and advise Internet marketers. And two of the most famous

Internet marketing experts in the country, Corey Rudl and Yanik Silver, are in my elite Platinum Inner Circle.

So, I want you to know that my comments that follow are 100% pragmatic. They come from "what works," not what I like or don't like.

Caught Up in the Web

Let's start with the escapee from Pandora's Box, the Internet.

From dot.com explosion to dot.com bust, plenty of companies, sales organizations, and individual sales professionals journeyed from seduced and mesmerized to disillusioned. The Internet is seductive technology and, at the moment, still a vastly over-hyped opportunity. However, there are a few legitimately useful Internet applications for sales pros.

It is important not to view the Internet as panacea, or for that matter, as significantly different from any other marketing media. It is another media, another tool. Not a replacement for anything.

It is also important not to be consumed by the Internet, but to control it and use it as a tool.

And it is important not to be threatened by the Web. Some businesses and some salespeople have been terrorized by its ability to commoditize, to facilitate price shopping. It does, in fact, have that capability, but it is only a valid threat to those dumb enough to be in a commoditizeable position.

How Smart Sales Professionals Use Web Sites

First of all, odds are your company has a lousy Web site. Most do. Most are institutional, image-y expansive brochures stuck up on the Web. So you are probably going to need your own site or sites.

One type of potentially useful site is for lead generation and/or lead capture, as described in detail in Chapter 18. If you can buy traffic online, use chat rooms, run banner ads, etc., then you can actually generate leads online. If your business is not well matched with this kind of online lead generation, it should probably still have a site for lead capture, for prospects driven online by offline marketing, whether from an ad, a letter, or something as simple as your .com address on your business card.

Another type of site is the aforementioned brochure or catalog online. Be careful of this, as it can do more harm than good. In many instances, this is a reference site for use by repeat customers, but it is inappropriate for acquiring new customers. For acquiring new business, a simple, bare-bones, sales letter site is usually more appropriate, especially a sales letter with a single focus, such as "selling" the appointment. My own main site, dankennedy.com, is a hybrid of these two.

Yet another type of site is a restricted-access site only for established clients or customers, through which you provide different kinds of added value.

Can you sell via a Web site? Actually, yes. One consultant who sells and provides high-priced training programs to corporate executives on the subject of finding, interviewing, choosing, and hiring the right employees uses his Web site like a PowerPoint presentation in concert with a phone conversation. The training contracts he sells may run between $15,000.00 and $150,000.00. Often, he has to attend a face-to-face meeting to secure the contracts. Increasingly though, when speaking with prospective clients on the phone, he asks if they can pop up his Web site at the same time. He then talks the prospective client through the Web site, somewhat like a salesperson might use a flip chart or flip book if sitting across the desk from the prospect. He is closing sales this way without leaving his office.

Earlier in this book, I talked about the use of tele-seminars for selling. In some fields where sophisticated Internet use is prevalent, selling is being done with "Webinars," conducted via Web sites.

The Trouble with Most Web Sites

Most sites are designed by techno-geeks and/or graphic artists who are not salespeople. They do not know how to sell. They do

My Platinum Inner Circle Member Yanik Silver is one of the top Internet marketing and sales experts and an astute analyst of direct-response copy. He offers Web-site analysis services. Visit NoBSwebcopy.com for information.

Keep these two things firmly in mind:

1. *Function over form.* Be clear about what you want the site to do for you, then design it or get it designed and built to do that job, nothing more.

2. *Control the visit.* Most Web designers give the site's visitors control over the visit, turning them loose to click here, go there, leap and hop, and wander around loose as much as they want. This is NOT the way to run a sales site.

not know when they are disrupting or destroying the selling process with their technological bells and whistles. They must be reigned in.

How Smart Sales Professionals Use E-Mail

I'll begin by telling you that, as I am writing this, there's been an explosion of e-mail delivery problems. Due to the nature of book publishing, what I write today about this subject may or may not still be true months later when you have this book in your hands. (That's why my monthly *No B.S. Marketing Letter* is very important to read.) Anyway, at the moment, a new federal anti-spam law—with "spam" very, very broadly defined—is kicking in. In addition, people have all sorts of e-mail screening gimmicks working for them. A lot of companies even have moats with alligators, beneath raised drawbridges; your e-mail sending address must be pre-approved, or your e-mail is unceremoniously dumped. There's more, but I won't bore you with all the grubby details. To be brief here, we can simply say that e-mail has a very high probability of never arriving or of being ignored when it does. Most Internet marketing advocates will not admit how unlikely it is that e-mail will gather positive attention; however, I have working relationships with six of the most famous such experts—and in amusing incongruity—they all extensively and increasingly use paper-and-ink direct-mail and telemarketing to sell their products, services, and seminars—even Web site design!

E-mail's greatest virtues are: that it is virtually instant and virtually free. I do not deny the virtues but caution that the benefits are real only when recipients welcome and read your e-mail. You have to carefully consider whether or not that can reasonably be presumed, situation by situation.

If a significant percentage of your clientele is online, they will want to be able to communicate with you by email, and you will want to accommodate them. You cannot, however, let the e-mail gates you open bury you in a time management crisis, and I have a lot to say about that in my *No B.S. Time Management* book.

E-mail auto-responders have largely replaced fax-on-demand as the most common means of instantly and automatically dispensing standard information to prospects or clients requesting it, as well as instantly confirming such requests or orders. You can set up "auto responders" that e-mail literature, sales letters, or other information back to your prospects and customers on request without you or any other person having to lift a finger. This can be a powerful tool in the right circumstances.

One caution about e-mail, however; direct-mail pros like me are still disturbed by the lack of control we as senders have over the look of the information, when it is received. When you use printed letters to prospect or to sell, cosmetic tricks such as underlining, bold facing, varying the size of the type, varying the typestyles, and adding handwritten margin notes are nearly as important as the copy itself. However, some of these tricks you can't (yet) do with e-mail, and others you can do but can't guarantee they won't be undone by the recipient's computer or printer. Simply put, you sacrifice a lot for the sake of speed and convenience of e-mail.

With that in mind, it's my contention that e-mail is better used for routine correspondence than for sales correspondence and better used for disseminating technical information than for selling. Further, I am opposed to it as replacement for other media. Instead, because it is free, I encourage my clients to add e-mail steps to a sequence, or keep unconverted leads in a follow-up program longer.

If you do want to aggressively use e-mail, especially in quantity, to reach out to new prospects, no one knows more about the science of getting it delivered, opened, read and responded to than my Platinum Member Corey Rudl. Corey's *Insider Secrets to E-Mail Marketing* is must reading.

How Some Entrepreneurs Create Massive Online Salesforces

My client and Platinum Member Yanik Silver built an online affiliate network of 22,262 people in less than 36 months, all selling his products via their Web sites, e-mail, and other means, all being tracked and paid their commissions automatically. Thanks to the power of this kind of affiliate marketing online, Yanik made more than a million dollars before the age of 30—all 100% on auto-pilot, without any direct contact with any customers. If you want to learn affiliate marketing, he's the guy to go to.

Laptop Computer Selling

These days, many sales representatives are reducing the number of samples, audiovisual equipment, or demonstration tools they schlep around with them, and are creating dynamic sales presentations thanks to their laptop or notebook portable computer. Graphs and charts formerly presented flat in flip books can now be rendered in three dimensions on the computer screen. Testimonials can come to life with photos or even full-motion video and sound. The workings of products such as industrial equipment can be demonstrated on the computer. And presentations can quickly and easily be personalized for each prospect in advance or during the presentation by plugging in information and making calculations. All this pretty much antiquates flip books, flip charts, portable videoplayers, and, of course, legal pads.

Even the carpet cleaners trained by Joe Polish use very sophisticated video presentations delivered on laptop computers in their prospects' homes.

A caution, though: as a professional speaker, I've watched similar technology invade this business. Presentations have gone high tech, with full-color computer graphics and PowerPoint multiple-screen presentations replacing overhead transparencies. When a truly accomplished and effective speaker chooses to use these tools to enhance a presentation, the results are sometimes very impressive.

But there are two risks: One, the mediocre or unprepared speaker may use these tools as crutches to disguise a poor presentation. Tools doth not a carpenter make. Two, the gizmos and techno-effects can be so dazzling they distract from the message. I've seen both risks realized many times. My belief is that a true pro can walk out onto a plain stage with nothing but his mind, mouth, and body and hold an audience spellbound and effectively communicate, persuade, and motivate without need of electronics. And most of the highest paid, most-in-demand, and best-known speakers in the country—such as my speaking colleagues Zig Ziglar, Jim Rohn, Tom Hopkins, and Brian Tracy—do just that.

Similarly, I think a true sales pro can command the attention, stimulate the interest, and secure the conviction of his prospect on the strength of his knowledge, "pitch," and enthusiasm— without reliance on special effects. If you need these things to function, then you are not functioning as well as you could and should be.

So, my "rules" are

- use these techno-wiz sales tools sparingly;
- use them for good reason, not just because they're available or because you think they're "cool";
- do not lazily rely on these tools to compensate for lack of knowledge, preparation, or selling skill.

Contact Management Tools

I'm a big believer in staying in constant and frequent communication with clients, targeted prospects, and other important contacts. If automating that process helps you to do it, I'm all for that—as long as you don't sacrifice the personal touch. For example, you can have your computer kick out e-mails or even regular letters to a list of clients every x-number of days. But none of that will ever substitute for you clipping an article from a magazine about fly fishing, jotting a handwritten note, and sending them to a client who is passionately interested in fly fishing.

There's plenty of off-the-shelf software in the contact management category that can cater to your needs. There are also specialists in this field who design and provide generic and customized contact management systems for sales professionals. Most of them routinely advertise in *Selling Power Magazine*, which every sales professional ought to be reading (check out www.sellingpower.com). John Paul Mendocha, Reed Hoisington, and Jeff Paul, all included in this book's Resource Directory, all have their own recommendations, which you may want to obtain and consider.

My client, Ron Romano, at Automated Marketing Solutions, is the ultimate "bundler" of, as his company name says, automated marketing solutions. There are tens of thousands of salespeople in diverse fields relying on his company for integrated Web sites; auto-responder-delivered sales literature in multistep, timed sequences; broadcast fax to the same leads; broadcast voice to the same leads; and more. One of AMS's top clients in the real estate field is one of the top performing agents in North America. This agent has over 500 leads a month generated by advertising and direct mail, all driven into an AMS-operated system, all sent more than two dozen different follow-up pieces, all without the agent ever doing one minute of work.

Still Can't Beat In-the-Flesh Selling

Admittedly, I am—by conditioning, preference, and age—a low-tech person in a high-tech world. This makes me cautious. For example, there are credible studies cropping up indicating that people who spend even a few hours a week on the Internet are more subject to depression than those who don't, and that people using the Internet for several hours every day are very subject to depression. Researchers theorize this has to do with the isolation of the medium. For me, this validates my own anxiety about stripping human relationships out of the process of doing business. I worry about the sales professionals who are so into automation that they actually achieve isolation.

There's a TV commercial where a company president calls his staff together, tells them they're losing customers, and that one they lost told him: "You just don't seem to care about us anymore." The president then starts handing out airline tickets telling everybody they are getting out of the office, into the field, and visiting all their accounts in person again—much to the groans and consternation of the troops. It's not a very good commercial because I can't for the life of me recall what it's selling; maybe an airline or a hotel chain. But I thought the scenario itself was profound.

The late Cavett Robert, founder of the National Speakers Association and one of the best salespeople I've ever known, was famous for his line: "They don't care how much you know until they know how much you care." Yep, it's trite. But it is NOT antiquated.

Prospects, customers, and clients at all levels—from the kitchen table to the corporate boardroom—still buy on emotion and justify with logic. They still must have an emotional, personal connection with a salesperson; they will not buy sophisticated or expensive goods and services from a vending machine. This should make you cautious about putting too much distance between yourself and your customer via technology.

Bonus
Book

Note: This small book was originally written for a private corporate client in 1993. It has been out of print for quite some time. I've been told used copies have changed hands on e-Bay for as much as $360.00. As I said earlier, I have made very minor changes to it mandated by time; however, 90% of what is printed here is the same as in the original edition.

If you have an especially strong interest in this subject, I would also recommend another book, which was sent to me by my Gold/VIP Member, a professional magician, Dave Dee. The book, titled *The Full Facts Book of Cold Reading,* is subtitled "A comprehensive guide to the most persuasive psychological manipulation technique in the world and its application to psychic readings." It is a detailed inside look at how professional psychics elicit information and do what are called "cold readings" of people. If you cannot find this in bookstores, try the author's Web site, www.ianrowland.com. I found it fascinating, accurate based on what I already knew, and valuable to enhance techniques I already use.

• • • • •

How To Read Anyone's Mind

Subvert Your Own Ego

Boy, are we vain! And, at the drop of a nickel, we'll be into the "can you top this game?" with anybody we're talking with. If the other person has an "I was so drunk" story, we've got a better one—if the other person has a sexual conquest story involving twins, we've got to trot out ours involving triplets. And, when we legitimately know more about something than the other person, we are compelled to demonstrate that superior knowledge.

This tendency must be suppressed if you are intent on learning as much as possible about a person from a particular conversation.

The ego is the enemy of communication anyway. The perfect path to other people's trust is the suppression of your ego so that theirs may shine.

The Easiest Way to Get Anybody to Confide in You Like their Most Trusted Friend—Fast

There is a classic persuasive marketing principle: people want most what they get the least of. And what most people get the least of is recognition, appreciation. This is as true of the most successful person you know as it is of the most "ordinary" person you know. At all levels of achievement, people are starved for recognition and appreciation. You can open a person up like magic by dispensing lots of these two things.

For example, the busiest man in the world will back off from his "busyness," have all his calls held, drop whatever he's doing to spend time with you and tell you everything you can think of asking—if you're very, very appreciative of how busy and important he is, of the time he makes for you.

When a person gives you some information, if you demonstrate appreciation for it and recognition of its value, guess what? That person will be eager to give more. I get a lot of free consulting and help from otherwise high-priced, busy experts with this strategy. I'll say something like: "You know, just that piece of information, that story's worth the price of lunch. I'm going to be able to use that...." And I'll describe the value the information has for me. What does this prompt? More disclosure. With this approach, I can get CEOs telling me their life stories and disclosing all the details of their businesses and finances in short order.

Keep in mind that everybody loves giving advice. Asking people for their opinions and their advice is a certain way to open them up and get them "spilling" what they know.

How To Ask Questions

1. Ask questions that cannot be answered "yes" or "no."
2. Preface with "what do you think about. . . ?" or "how do you feel about. . . ?"
3. Form an extension question by repeating key words. For example:

   Wife: "You seem preoccupied. Is anything wrong?"
   Husband: "No."
   Wife: "There must be something."
   Husband: "Just a little trouble with the boss."
   Wife: "Trouble with the boss?"

4. Start with questions that are easy to answer.

5. Exchange information—don't relentlessly interrogate.
6. Stimulate further disclosure by agreeing when you can.

Study Good Interviewers

Here's your opportunity to watch television with a purpose. Many talk show hosts are very skilled interviewers, adept at getting their guests to "reveal themselves." Barbara Walters, Dick Cavett, Johnny Carson, Larry King, and Oprah Winfrey are exceptionally talented interviewers.

When you watch these and other hosts/interviewers, take note of the things they do repetitively and consistently. Look for the skill behind the style, the thing that is done so consistently it must be "principle."

Determine That You Will Learn Something from Everybody

This is an attitude that is particularly useful in getting information from others—a firm conviction that there is something to be learned from everyone and a determination to learn something from everyone.

As with most things, attitude is at least as important as aptitude, if not more important. This simple mindset will draw people to you and motivate them to open up to you.

Listening Skills

You probably know that the inability to listen accurately and effectively costs this country billions and billions of dollars annually. There are big problems: defense contractor cost overruns, airplane crashes, all sorts of mistakes made in business and industry, because even when one person insists the message was delivered correctly, it was heard wrong. There are little productivity problems, too. And business and personal relationship destruction. And students' poor grades. And on and on—all because, although enormous investments are made throughout our childhood and adult lives to teach us how to speak and how to write, very little is done to teach us how to listen.

I read a very interesting article years ago, where a number of prostitutes were interviewed. Many said that many of their "regulars" often paid not for sex, they didn't even have sex—but for someone to listen to them. Just recently, I saw a *Geraldo* show featuring operators of 900-number/800-number "phone sex" businesses who said the same thing—many regulars call and do not engage in explicit sex talk but instead talk about the day they had, their frustrations at work or at home, etc. In other words, they pay for someone who will listen to them. This is just one of many situations that has convinced me that REAL listening is a rarity, and therefore immensely valuable and marketable.

Active Listening

To listen effectively and ACTIVELY, I think you need to do all these things.

L = LIKE
You have to find some thing(s) to honestly like about the other person.

I = INTEREST
You have to instantly cultivate a sincere interest, either in the other person or in the content of what the other person is saying.

For example, I'll pay attention to, say, Crandall, the CEO of American Airlines if I see him on a talk show. I'm interested in what he's saying because I travel a lot, and because I'm in business but not because he is a particularly interesting person. I'll pay attention to what Gregory Hines is saying on a talk show, not because I'm interested in tap dancing but because he is an interesting, passionate person.

S = SEE

You have to really extend yourself sometimes to see the other person's point of view, to visualize the background and causes of the person's thinking. You have to use your mind's eye for greater understanding.

T = TOUCH

You have to let yourself be "touched" and, as the phone company says, "reach out and touch" the other person; let there be emotional linkage. If you try to keep yourself distant and uninvolved, the other person will sense it, respond by mirroring, and crawl into a protective shell.

E = ENGAGE

You must take some initiative and be actively involved without taking away control from the other person. Display your involvement by nodding, displaying attentive posture and other body language, asking brief questions, agreeing when possible, and asking nonoffensive devil's advocate type questions.

N = NEED

You have probably heard the phrase "need to know," as in "We'll tell them on a 'need to know' basis." I suggest operating on a

NEED to know basis; you have such a thriving, thirsty curiosity about what makes people tick that you really need to know as much about other people as you need to breathe. This creates clearly sincere enthusiasm for what others tell you, encouraging them to tell you more.

ACTIVE LISTENING means that, overall, you are as involved in a conversation as the person doing most of the talking. Leaning forward, nodding, appropriate facial expressions, taking notes in business setting, all help you listen and convey interest. The most important part of all, though, is "total concentration."

To be able to totally concentrate, you have to first do what *Psycho-Cybernetics* author Dr. Maxwell Maltz called "clearing the calculator." Most little hand-held calculators have to be "cleared" of one problem before they can work on another. You have to do this mentally. You may use meditation, self-hypnosis, the Silva Method, whatever. But there is nothing more flattering or compelling than totally concentrating on another person's personality.

The Technique of "Displayed Interest"

Every one of us has, at least once, had the experience of meeting and spending time with someone who displayed such rapt fascination with us that we wound up telling them the most amazing things about ourselves—we so enjoyed being with them we sought to prolong the meeting. Many times, this is courtship behavior. We fall in love with the person of the opposite sex who seems to be unendingly fascinated with us!

I was reminded of this not long ago, when meeting with the owner of a public relations firm that I was considering hiring. She was fascinated with me. She was so focused on me a bomb could have gone off without disturbing her concentration. I was completely captivated by her nonverbal flattery. It was only after the meeting that I logically analyzed what had just happened, how I'd been mesmerized, how I'd wound up talking so much about me.

It's this kind of "displayed interest" that can get people to tell you everything about themselves.

I Will Never Forget...

...a young lady I knew only as a business acquaintance whipping out one of her newly remodeled breasts for my inspection. What could provoke such behavior? In thinking it over afterward, I became convinced it was nothing more (or less) than my being an extraordinarily good listener to a person desperate for attention and consideration. It is only one of many of what I consider to be amazing incidents that have happened to me while I've been practicing the art and science of listening.

Most people go through their daily lives with others only "surface listening" to them. I experience this constantly myself, and so do you. People ask us how things are going or how we are, without wanting to know or waiting to hear anything more than "fine" or "OK." Most people "listen" while doing other things—walking, shuffling paper, whatever. At home, dinner conversation is replaced by the TV trays in front of the tube, and I'm guilty of that too. After a period of time of this, a person becomes remarkably vulnerable to anybody who stops, digs in, and really listens. A great cause of unhappiness in many peoples' lives is the absence of anyone who is thoroughly fascinated with them and what they're all about. Filling this void gives you access, even control.

What Does "Reading Between the Lines" Really Mean?

You've heard the phrase—"you have to read between the lines"—but what does that really mean? When people talk or write, they *communicate two ways at the same time*: with EXPLICIT messages and IMPLICIT messages. Explicit is the actual, as-stated message. Implicit is the "extra message" implied by voice inflection, body language, punctuation, etc.

Just as an example, has someone ever said to you, "If I were you, I would…." Or, has someone said, "I don't care where we go for lunch. Chinese would be great, but I'm up for anything." In both cases, there is an implicit or extra message quite different from the explicit message. And, in both cases, there is an attempt at manipulative control. In the first example, the person really means: here's what to do. In the second, the person really wants Chinese.

Discipline yourself to ALWAYS listen for the implicit or extra message.

Incidentally, the less secure a person is, in general or in a particular situation, the more likely he'll communicate his true thoughts through these extra messages rather than his exact words.

Eye Contact

At conventions or trade shows I sometimes catch myself committing this "communication sin:" carrying on a conversation with one person while frequently glancing around, watching for other people I know and need to talk to. Maybe it's forgivable in the trade show environment, but it's still discourteous to the other person and, more importantly, a huge impediment to total communication.

Maintaining total, unwavering eye contact with the other person gives you incredible power. This is another aspect of active listening, of displayed interest, of flattery, all of which contributes to the other person's desire to confide in you. Also, because "the eyes are the windows to the soul," you gain an intuitive sense of the other person via the eye contact.

Body Language

You probably remember "body language" as kind of a business fad. For a while, everybody was writing about body language, everybody was talking about body language. It was "hot." Then the business public moved its attention to the next panacea, and body language was pretty much forgotten. If you find a book on body language at the bookstore today, it'll be buried on a bottom shelf with dust on it.

However, the topic is as valid as ever.

We communicate much more and much more openly nonverbally than we do verbally. Even while our lips lie, our physical movements generally tell the truth. (Some people have a real problem matching their facial expressions and other physical movement with what they're saying, so that others—although they may not realize it consciously—feel uncomfortable subconsciously and may not trust the speaker.)

You can use an understanding of body language two ways. One is in the reading of others' minds. You can use it to tell when the person across the desk has "bought" your idea. If there are ten women at the bar, you can tell which one is eager to be asked to dance. If you're a speaker, and there are 20 people in the front row, you can tell which one is alone. In an office setting, you can determine when someone is really "in a good mood," so you can approach them with your idea or request.

The second use of an understanding of body language is in reinforcing and empowering your own verbal communication. You can first make sure that your physical movements and facial expressions are congruent with what you're saying and how you're saying it. Then, you can go beyond that and make your physicality communicate on a level by itself. There are masters at this. If you watch the *Personal Power/Tony Robbins* TV infomercial with the sound turned off, you'll still pick up a certain positive, intriguing energy from Tony throughout the show. But if you watch many other people being interviewed, regrettably, myself included, that energy doesn't shine through. Glenn Turner has a particular body movement he makes during the course of a motivational speech, hooked to an especially compelling and persuasive point, that draws the audience's attention, pulls them toward him, actually moves them to the edges of their seats.

In one-on-one selling, I've learned there's a physical "way" that communicates neediness to the other person and drives away sales. There's a different physical "way" that communicates complete dispassion about whether or not the sale gets made that draws sales in. For want of a better way to describe it, the "relaxed" body language wins every time.

In Johnny Carson's closing broadcast, he brought a stool out on stage and sat down, to talk to the studio audience and viewers at home—I think this was the first time he had ever sat down on a stool on stage. Why did he do that? That action instantly and communicated: "Tonight is very different and very special, and I'm going to deal with it and you differently, more intimately than ever before. I'm not going to talk at you; I'm going to share with you" more effectively than if he had said all that a hundred times over.

If you want to end a conversation, you can hasten the other person along with certain body language. If you don't mind annoying the other person, looking at your watch is the blatant version of this.

We can convey what's on our minds and discover what's on others' minds with body language, and I suggest blowing the dust off the old body language books and making a fresh study of this topic would be a very useful thing to do.

Mirroring

Tony Robbins has "popularized" this, but it's not anything new. The Amazing Kreskin, a mind-reader by profession, wrote this back in 1984:

> The ideal rapport is a mirror image of those you're confronting. Let them see their best selves in you. If you're talking to someone who's bombastic, be pleasantly bombastic, but not competitive. If the person is shy and soft-spoken, reflect that tone in yourself…there's a little of everyone else inside each of us, and the challenge is to find what in us is in tune with the other person and reflect it.

Each of us has a particular way of speaking, a cadence, a speed, a vocabulary. Most of us appreciate a particular kind of humor—we don't necessarily laugh at the same jokes that our neighbor does. Being in tune means reflecting these aspects of the other person.

Even your physical presence can enhance or detract from rapport. I'm quick to remove the tie and jacket and roll up shirt sleeves the instant I sense my audience is in a casual mood.

I study the other person's gestures. Does he use his hands a lot? If so, I do too. If not, then I won't either.

Simply, people accept, trust, and spill their guts to people who they see themselves in. I've often done very well with hugely successful, entrepreneurial men who created their success out of dust, struggled, failed, recovered, made it through hard work and hustle—because they see themselves in me. Conversely, I have a rough time dealing with corporate, middle management bureaucrats who've gone from college to corporate environment and are better at office politics than anything else because they cannot see any of them reflected in me. But, when you really understand this, you can identify some "thing" about just about everybody you can mirror.

Humor is a great mirroring opportunity. Recently, I was the odd man out, the new dynamic in a group of five people who had already been working together and been at several meetings together. Although the others were not in sync themselves, their corporate-political tendency was to unite in fear and resistance against me, the "outsider." As I sat there that morning, hoping for an opportunity to create rapport with somebody, the fifth guy rolled into the meeting room and told everybody a joke. In this case, it was a macho, coarse, "blue" joke, a locker-room joke. This told me a lot about that guy. Among other things, I decided to be a little "earthy" in my language, particularly when agreeing with or piggybacking on this guy's comments. It wasn't long before he "bought me," became my ally, nodded approvingly when I made a point.

I'll tell you something very interesting about all this, hopefully in a way that is not offensive to anybody. I have a number of friends in the hair styling/hair salon industry, including a woman I've been friends with for many years—in fact, we dated between my marriages. Most of the men in her salon and, in my observation, in the industry, are openly gay. Women love these guys. They attach themselves to them, they confide in them, they tell them the most amazing things. We've talked about this, and both conclude that the reason is mirroring; these gay men mirror the women.

There's a fine line here to be aware of. I do not suggest becoming a total chameleon, changing to match the other person like a chameleon changes colors to match his environment. That's going too far. You have to be you; there has to be a core personality that is a constant. But short of cutting into that core personality, you can learn to modify your approach, to "lean" in the same direction as the other person you're working with at the moment.

The example of speed of speaking is a good one. Slowing or accelerating your speed of speaking is certainly not the same as compromising your personality. But it can be very helpful in making the other person comfortable.

When you meet a new person for the first time, that person instantly provides a "snapshot" of what they're comfortable with—through speed of speaking, posture, gestures—and you can immediately make some modifications in yourself to mirror the other person. I think of it as about a 20% adjustment—80% of me stays constant, 20% tries to adapt, to mirror the other person I'm dealing with.

The Right Image

Your "outer package" does have an impact on how quickly and easily people accept you, trust you, relax with you, and reveal themselves to you.

I can tell you for a fact, for example, that chiropractors who meet with new patients dressed "like a doctor" will get farther, faster, than the chiropractor who insists on being "casual." There are occupational biases, geographic biases, all sorts of biases, and you can use them to your advantage or fight them—your choice.

Nido Qubein is a very successful consultant and friend of mine. The joke about Nido at the National Speakers Association conventions is "You'll find Nido in the pool—easy to spot—only guy in there in a three-piece pin striped suit." Nido deals almost exclusively with Fortune 1000 clients, and he has recognized that those people will be most comfortable with him if he looks, in every way, like one of them—or even a slightly superior version of them. In his case, he's both "mirroring" and meeting their expectations.

There are, of course, exceptions, contradictions—you can have great influence by appearing totally contrary to expectations. I'd imagine Gary Halbert has that occur. I know Dick Sutphen has it happen. But you have to be "set up" very, very well for this to work.

The safer, surer approach is to meet expectations, and when appropriate, mirror.

Be Prepared

I'm amazed at the people who go into sales calls, negotiations, meetings, etc., wholly unprepared, either "winging it" or applying the same "canned" procedure to everybody. This is fine if you're selling a nickel-and-dime commodity, but if you're dealing in the "Important," it's best to be as prepared as possible.

A lot of the people I deal with have written books or been the subject of books, tapes, or newspaper or magazine articles; or know somebody who knows me. Before a meeting, I'll delve into as much of this as I can to get a "feel" for that person. For my high-priced seminars, I ask attendees to complete and turn in detailed questionnaires in advance, so I can get that feel for them before actually meeting them. From this kind of information, I'm often able to correctly anticipate how a particular person thinks, how they're "wired."

Observe

I like meeting with people in their environments because their environments reveal a lot about them.

An office with a wall full of plaques and certificates says something very different than an office with a wall full of photographs of people, doesn't it? I deal with several former pro athletes. One has an office virtually devoid of memorabilia from his sports career. Another has an office full of footballs, trophies, photographs of teammates, and so on. What do these two offices communicate? I initially gambled and was proved right in deducing that the first person's office says he has decided to put his sports career behind him; in fact, he is eager to shed his jock past and be known for his entrepreneurial accomplishments. Talking sports with this guy is a mistake; ignoring sports entirely and zeroing in on business discussion is correct. The second fellow still clings to and relies on his on-field accomplishments and celebrity. He is comfortable with that and still uncomfortable with the business world. Asking him for an autographed ball is the right thing to do.

There's a scene in the movie *Shining Through* where Michael Douglas asks Melanie Griffith to close her eyes and recall what she has noticed about his office. It's a good test. When you go into a new environment, challenge yourself to be so observant that you can close your eyes after a minute and recall a lot of detail about the office. Then analyze what that office has to say about its occupant.

The Chink In the Armor

Everybody, no matter how successful, has at least one "chink in the armor," and knowing about it may help you better deal with that person. Often—in fact, more often than not—the chink relates to self-esteem.

For example, I have one client and friend who is a very, very successful, smart, capable businesswoman in the top 5% income bracket in the United States, and probably in the top 5% in her particular profession. On the surface, she is understandably very confident and independent. But deep down she is remarkably "hung up" on the fact that she did not attend college and her feelings about this "lack" inhibit her and affect her in surprising ways. Another individual I deal with is, again, enormously successful professionally, but is largely disliked by his peers, not respected by his staff, and totally taken for granted by his spouse. This guy is starved for recognition. I have a client who has had several years of remarkable success after years of struggle, and he is terrified that it's going to end tomorrow. Can you see how being aware of the chinks in these peoples' armor makes it easier to help them— if you're into helping them—or sell to them; to manipulate them? To predict how they will respond to a particular idea or situation?

Five Human Characteristics that Can Be Relied On: What Are People Thinking?

1. Resistance to Change

Yes, people can be motivated to accept—even welcome—change, but, initially, the instant reaction to any and all proposed or perceived change is resistance. This reaction occurs for a variety of reasons, including fear, inconvenience, laziness, and territorial protectiveness.

2. *Wandering Attention*

People have limited and decreasing attention spans. They lack the ability and know-how to concentrate. Their attention can easily be attracted by anything that is pleasurable, exciting, or entertaining. The more complex the idea you are presenting, the more certain wandering attention is. Therefore, at any given moment, you can bet the other person is thinking about personal concerns, a "to-do" list, a sexual fantasy, just about anything but the subject at hand.

3. *Wishful Listening*

People have the uncanny ability to hear what they want to hear, not what is being said. And they'll later swear they heard what they believe they heard.

4. *Jumped-to Conclusions*

People are impatient, so, rather than hearing another person out, they'll often mentally cut off the speaker and make an assumption about everything being said.

5. *Habitual Negative Thinking*

Most people think mostly negative thoughts. Their first reaction will be to see the negative, the difficult, the impossible, and the unpleasant aspects of something.

When you keep in mind that these five characteristics largely control the way a person is thinking most of the time, it becomes ridiculously easy to "predict" specific thoughts and reactions in a particular situation. If using this for persuasive purposes, you then want to prepare with all this in mind and try to control these elements rather than letting them control the outcome.

How Physical Characteristics Affect a Person's Thinking

It's my belief that short men are more aggressive, meaner if in power, and more bullyish than tall men. Overweight men are more easily intimidated and more motivated by a desire for acceptance, recognition, and respect than men of average weight. Blonde, very attractive women are most eager to demonstrate their intellect, to be asked for their opinions on important matters. Women are much more observant than men, so a man's dress and appearance is more important when meeting with a woman than when meeting with a man. A woman wearing a lot of jewelry is easily influenced by flattery; a woman wearing little or no jewelry will be turned off by casual flattery.

All this is stored in my memory bank. I don't think about it much, consciously; in fact, I had to work at dragging it out for this book, but it is there, and it does influence my behavior with these types of people.

What observations have you made about how physical characteristics are predictive of thinking and behavior?

Sure, these are generalizations, biases. And I know that they are subject to attack as oversimplifications and certainly subject to exception. But I ask that you keep in mind that I deal, in one-on-one situations, with dozens of different people each week, a thousand or so a year, and, in groups, tens of thousands more. And I believe I have sufficient evidence to draw and reasonably rely on these conclusions. When you consider the pace most of us are on these days, the speed at which we meet, greet, interact with, and move on, the use of pigeon-holing—of quickly categorizing people—is virtually essential.

Demographic Clues to Attitudes

People born and raised in the Midwest are more trusting and trustworthy than those raised in California.

How do you feel about that statement? Sure, it's unfair. There certainly are very trustworthy people born, raised, and living in California. I have one or two such clients there myself who have the highest imaginable integrity. And certainly there are some people of zero integrity born and raised in Kansas, Indiana, and Ohio. But, setting aside the individual cases and deliberately trying to develop a generalization that is truer than false, I'd bet on this one.

Let's stay with California for a second. Image and appearance is more important there than anywhere else in the United States. People in Los Angeles are much more likely to quickly form very firm conclusions about you based on the car you drive, clothes you wear, and whether or not you have a cell phone than people in, say New Orleans or Indianapolis. If you're going to do business in L.A., you'd better get a grip on this.

People raised in high-income families will have very different values and opinions than people raised in low-income families. People living in major metropolitan cities respond differently than those living in small towns to just about everything. For example, there's less cynicism in small-town residents than in city dwellers. People with children—parents—certainly respond differently than do married couples who do not have children.

In marketing to groups or people, we consider their demographic commonalities. When we can, we'll deliver a very different marketing message for the same product to a group of 45-year-olds from Rhode Island than to 35-year-olds in Atlanta. And, different demographic groups are drawn to different products—for the most part, the women who regularly read *Cosmopolitan* are different than those who regularly read *Redbook;*

the men who read *Playboy* different from those who read *Hustler.* Because all this applies to marketing to groups, why wouldn't it apply to influencing individuals?

I try to get a "demographic profile" in my mind of the person I'm working with—what are the "vital statistics"?—age, income, marital and family status, hometown, educational background, etc. I ask myself, Who else do I know who closely matches that demographic profile? What is that person like?

I happen to know a guy very, very well who is the demographic clone of H. Ross Perot, the Texas businessman who ran for president in 1992 and 1996. They both got their early entrepreneurial experience delivering newspapers on horseback. Their upbringing—virtually identical. I mean, their backgrounds are virtually interchangeable. As a result, watching Perot as a presidential candidate was especially interesting to me. I knew what Perot was going to say before he said it. When Marilyn Quayle, wife of then Vice President Dan Quayle, attacked him on the *Today Show,* I knew instantly how Perot would react and what he'd say. There's a technical term for this: "demographic overlay." If you can do a demographic overlay, you can quickly read someone's mind.

The Biggest Difference: "Think" vs. "Feel"

There is a substantial amount of very good, very interesting, and very sophisticated literature out there about the importance of communicating differently with men than with women, and you can make a study of all this if you like. But the shorthand shortcut is that most (not all) males respond primarily on a "thinking" level; most (not all) women respond primarily on a "feeling" level: "how do you *feel* about that" vs. "what do you *think* about that?"

If you want to achieve open communication, making this single adjustment and staying on the appropriate think/feel "channel" is very important.

I'd add that women generally, and probably correctly, trust their "intuition"—instincts, subconscious mind's opinions, whatever you want to call it—much more than men do. Whether they ever analytically sort it out or not, women seem more tuned into nonverbal communication, to confidence; they've got better built-in truth detectors than we do. (Except when "blinded" in a romantic relationship.)

Be an Informed, Interesting Person

You have to be able to talk with people about what interests them before you can get them to open up to you.

I once built a very good relationship with a banker by getting involved with his obsession with fly fishing. I didn't know a damned thing about fishing when we met, but when I discovered the incredible commitment he had to his hobby, I went and got educated very quickly.

As a general rule, the more you know about a broad, diverse range of "stuff," the better. I have a client who loves horse racing—it so happens, I know a lot about horse racing, so, as Joan Rivers says, "we can talk." I have another client who's very into the theater. Before I visit with her, I make sure to get a copy of *The New Yorker* and the Sunday *New York Times* to get caught up on what's going on in the theater, so "we can talk." I have a client who is very involved with…well, you get the idea. I suppose in any given month, I read dozens of trade and specialty magazines, watch TV programs, and seek other sources of information dealing with subjects of interest to a client.

I want to be informative AND entertaining. Compare the salaries of Jay Leno with a college dean, by the way, and you'll instantly know which of the two is most important.

How To Know When a Person's Resistance Is Irrational

The signs of irrational opposition are as follows:

- *Vehemence.* If a person expresses his disagreement with more intensity and excitement than the situation seems to warrant, he's lost control. He may even be fighting an internal battle that has nothing much to do with you.
- *Stone-walling.* A person who is unresponsive, refuses to discuss or debate, or ask questions has put up a stone wall of opposition.
- *Irrelevance.* A person who introduces irrelevant arguments and goes off on tangents is trying to change the subject.
- *Objection Ping-Pong.* This person plays games with you, introducing an objection, then after it's answered, trots out another objection, then another, then another.
- *Paranoia.* A paranoid person trots out a collection of "worst case scenarios."

When these behaviors occur, know that any attempt at logical persuasion will be thwarted. Your choices are (a) to extricate yourself, retreat, and return to persuade another day, or (b) risk confronting the person about the behavior and asking for the real, hidden reasons for the resistance.

It is, incidentally, almost impossible to change the mind of "the true believer," who uses all five of these to stay linked to the chosen belief. If you want to understand this type of unshakeability and/or you are involved in creating believers—i.e., members, customers, recruits, etc., THE book to get and study is Eric

Hoffer's *The True Believer*. This book explains everything from David Duke to Ross Perot to Amway to Jim and Tammy Bakker.

F.O.R.M.

I teach this to people involved in multi-level network marketing as the process for breaking the ice with strangers, getting conversations going, and very quickly finding out what's most important to a person. But it'll work for anybody, not just a network marketer.

FORM is an acronym, to help you remember the four things to ask everybody about.

F—STANDS FOR FAMILY

For some people, family is THE most important thing in their life, and the path to fast rapport is ooh-ing and aah-ing over the snapshots of kids and grandkids.

O—STANDS FOR OCCUPATION

For many people, their business or career is either their greatest area of pain or greatest area of joy, and expressing interest in that is like turning on a faucet.

R—STANDS FOR RECREATION

Some people live for their hobbies. Golfers, fishermen, and photographers, for example, are rabid about these activities.

M—STANDS FOR MONEY

A lot of people are extremely interested in everything related to money. If they see an art object in your home, they can't help but wonder what you paid for it. I'll always remember being in an adult nightclub (topless dancing establishment) with a group of entrepreneurs, noticing that the most successful guy had wandered off, and finding him back in the dressing (or "undressing") room, sitting, surrounded by mostly naked, attractive women, studiously asking questions about gross sales, average tab, tips, and other financial statistics.

Each individual is more interested in one of these areas of life than the other three. Once you isolate which area a person is most interested in, you can often accurately predict what he's thinking in response to certain stimulus.

For example, take four guys hearing a news item about a very successful baseball player's new contract. "F" thinks: my kid's got an arm like a rocket. I hope he grows up and makes the majors. "O" thinks: what a dumb job, running around playing a kid's game. "R" thinks: oughta get some of the guys together and play some ball this weekend. "M" thinks: geez, two mil a year! I wonder how much that works out to each time at bat?

Similarly, when you make ANY statement, the other person "processes" it "through" his primary interest in life, family, occupation, recreation or money.

The Power of Suggestion

Some people bought this book not out of a desire to "read" others' minds but, instead, to "control" others' minds. Without passing judgment, let me tell you that, to a great degree, you can do exactly that, if that is your chief aim. To control a GROUP of people, study Eric Hoffer's book *The True Believer*. Probably without intending to, he provided a very practical, precise method for gaining control over a room full or a nation full of people.

To control or direct an individual's thoughts, rely on the single power of suggestion. For starters, lock this principle into your mind: people translate the words they hear into pictures, think in pictures, and are most readily led by pictures.

If I say to you, "If you die, will you leave your family penniless and in poverty?", you automatically get a picture in your mind. Now that may be a classic, Depression-era picture of a woman and a couple urchins, in scruffy clothes, sitting on a doorstep. Or it might be a gleeful picture of your cheating, bitching, ungrateful wife bursting into tears at the reading of your will. It will be a picture, but I have exerted little control over what the picture will be. I could further suggest the nature of the picture, couldn't I? And that's the "trick"—to deliberately extend the suggestion.

If I say: "Let's take a week off and go to a beach somewhere," I'm again leaving the picture at risk. You may conjure up a positive, persuasive scene of you on a beach, getting a tan, watching gorgeous girls in skimpy bikinis, etc. Or you may pull up the very memorable picture of your last trip to Mexico—sunburn, stomach virus, and all. But if I fully detail my picture, I can make it your picture. If I say: "Let's take a week off, go to the beach, get a couple of hammocks in good positions, a cooler of drinks, some good books, leave the cell phones locked up at home, and really relax. . . and I know just the place, where there'll be a good breeze, pure white sand, clear water, and lots of great looking women. . . ." What pictures are you forming in your mind now?

Try this exercise. Find a quiet, comfortable place to sit. Sit down and clear your mind as best you can. Now think back to the last time you took a good, bracing hot shower—maybe this morning—and concentrate on your fingers and hands, the hot water splashing over them. Switch to starting and building a fire. See yourself rubbing your hands together over that great fire, soaking in the warmth.

It won't be long before your hands actually get warmer. The power of suggestion is so great that most people can raise or lower their entire body temperature or any part of their body by 10 to 15 degrees purely through mental imagery. There is a physiological reaction to a psychological exercise.

Cavett Robert said "people won't buy burial plots unless they see the hearse parked at the door." He oughta know—he made a fortune teaching people how to sell burial insurance. And the key word there is *"see."* So your job is to speak in a way that conveys the right pictures. Know that everything you say will become pictures—the question is: what pictures?

When I say, from the front of the room in my marketing seminars, "Think about what it would be like to get up each and every morning KNOWING, absolutely knowing, exactly how many calls you will receive that day, from new prospects ready and eager to do business with you. What would that feel like? How would you like to live that way?" I'm hoping for some very definite pictures—that the person in the audience sees herself getting up spryly, eagerly, rather than crawling out of bed; smiling into the mirror; maybe answering the phone and getting a pleasant call from a customer. But whenever time permits, I go ahead and add: "I'll bet you'd get out of bed a little differently than you do some mornings now. I'll bet you'd jump up and say 'Good morning, God!' instead of 'Good God, it's morning.' I'll bet you'd give that mirror a big smile." This is suggestion at work.

Now, any good hypnotist or hypnotherapist will tell you that some people are more "suggestible" than others, so this works differently with different people. And it's rare that anybody gets so good at using the power of suggestion that he can literally, totally control another person's responses. But make no mistake about it, everybody has some degree of receptivity to this type of suggestion, and anybody can learn to use this power.

Essential
Reading

Bodybusiness by Ken Cooper, AMACOM

Getting Through to People by Jesse Nirenberg, Reward Books

Secrets of the Amazing Kreskin by Kreskin, Prometheus Books

Use Both Sides of Your Brain by Tony Buzan, Plume Books

Unlimited Power by Anthony Robbins, Fawcett

The True Believer by Eric Hoffer, Dimension

Summary of
Key Strategies

1. Don't "show off." Let the other person have the spotlight. Subvert your ego.
2. Give lots of recognition and appreciation.
3. Show appreciation for the value of the information given to you by the other person.
4. Build the other person up—ADD to his or her self-esteem.
5. Be a cheerful person.
6. Maintain a healthy sense of humor.
7. Avoid the "feel" of interrogation.
8. Reveal yourself (to get others to reveal themselves).
9. Learn to creatively structure your questions.
10. Emulate others who ask questions effectively.
11. Have the "learner" attitude.
12. Listen ACTIVELY.
13. Totally concentrate.
14. SHOW your interest.

15. Realize that just about everybody has a great emotional need to be listened to.
16. Be alert for the "extra messages."
17. Maintain eye contact.
18. Learn to read body language.
19. Learn to "speak" body language.
20. Use specific body language to set up and assist special communication situations. (Johnny Carson example.)
21. Learn to "mirror."
22. Present the most effective image.
23. Prepare.
24. Invade the other person's environment and be observant. (Thinking leaves clues.)
25. Look for the chink in the armor.
26. Play the odds. Bet that basic human characteristics are at work.
27. You CAN judge a book by its cover.
28. Consider the person's demographics.
29. Motivate women differently than men and vice versa.
30. Use FORM to discover the person's main area of interest.
31. Know a little about a lot of different things.
32. Think twice about trying to accomplish anything with a person who is clearly irrational.
33. Use the power of suggestion.

Resource
Directory

This directory will give you information to contact the people and access the resources listed throughout this book. In this directory, you will find many of the people listed chapter by chapter, based on the first reference to them in the book. The many marketing advisors and consultants who are providing training and systems based on my "Magnetic Marketing" to specific niche industries and professions are at the end of the directory, organized by industry.

Chapter 1

Maltz, Dr. Maxwell. The late Dr. Maltz was the father of "self-image psychology," and his original book *Psycho-Cybernetics* has sold more than 30 million copies worldwide. Dan Kennedy and several associates acquired rights to all Dr. Maltz's works, and in recent years, Kennedy has co-authored *The New Psycho-Cybernetics* book, *The New Psycho-Cybernetics* audio program by Nightingale-Conant, and the *Zero Resistance Selling* book. Psycho-Cybernetics is, in essence, a scientific approach with practical mental training techniques to improve all aspects of personal performance. www.psycho-cybernetics.com.

Ziglar, Zig. One of America's most popular, celebrated motivational speakers for three generations, Zig's book *See You At The Top* is a true classic. www.zigziglar.com

Chapter 4

Stone, W. Clement. Recommended book: *The Success System that Never Fails.*

Chapter 6

Hill, Napoleon. Recommended books: *Think and Grow Rich* and *Succeed and Grow Rich Through Persuasion.*

Chapter 10

Carson, Mitch. Impact Products. Phone: 888-215-4758 or visit Web site: www.impactproducts.com.

Luttrell, Rel. Phone: 870-862-8802/fax: 870-862-4835 or visit Web site: www.imageone.com.

Warren, B. Shawn. Phone: 502-459-1440/fax: 502-361-2783 or visit Web site: www.fratline.com.

Chapter 12

Tolleson, Tracy. Visit Web site: www.tracytolleson.com.

Chapter 14

Hoisington, Reed. Phone: 910-484-4519/fax: 910-485-3524.

Nicholas, Ted. Phone: +44-171-432-0384/fax: +44-171-432-0516 (in London, U.K.)

Chapter 16

Harrison, Stephen, and Bill. Phone: 800-989-1400/fax: 610-284-3704 or visit Web site: www.freepublicity.com.

Hartunian, Paul. Phone: 973-509-5244/fax: 973-509-1833 or visit Web site: www.hartunian.com.

Chapter 17

Marshall, Perry. Phone: 708-788-4461/fax: 708-788-4599 or visit Web site: www.perrymarshall.com.

Chapter 20

Romano, Ron. Automated Marketing Solutions. Phone: 800-858-8889/fax: 800-858-5753 or visit Web site: www.findmeleads.com.

Chapter 21

Mendocha, John Paul. SpeedSelling seminars and coaching programs. Phone: 909-783-4400/fax: 909-370-1170 or visit Web site: www.speedselling.net.

Chapter 22

ATG Technologies/Pat Live. Phone: 800-775-7790.

Fatt, Rory. Restaurant Marketing Systems. Phone: 604-940-6900/fax: 604-940-6902.

Chapter 23

Rudl, Corey. Phone: 604-730-2833/fax: 604-638-6015

Silver, Yanik. Phone: 301-770-0423/fax: 301-770-1096 or visit the Web site www.surefiremarketing.com.

Marketing Advisors by Industry

AUTO REPAIR

Ron Ipach/CinRon Marketing. Phone: 513-860-1300/fax: 513-860-3494 or visit Web site: www.cinron.com.

CARPET CLEANERS

Joe Polish/Piranha Marketing. Phone: 480-858-0008/fax: 480-858-0004 or visit Web site www.joepolish.com.

INSURANCE AGENTS

Jeff Paul. Phone: 630-778-0018/fax: 630-778-0019.

Dean Cipriano. Phone: 856-769-5050/fax: 856-769-5055.

Pamela Yellen. Phone: 505-466-1167/fax: 505-466-2167.

CHIROPRACTORS

Dr. Ben Altadonna. Phone: 925-314-9669/fax: 925-891-3851.

COMMERCIAL/PROPERTY/CASUALTY INSURANCE AGENTS

Michael Jans. Phone: 541-593-7464/fax: 360-397-0170.

DENTISTS

Jerry Jones, Jones Direct. Phone: 503-371-1390/fax: 503-371-1299.

Dr. Bob Willis. Phone: 918-298-8239/fax: 918-298-7943.

Dr. Chris Brady. Phone: 719-495-3168/fax: 719-730-3600.

Dr. Tom Orent. Phone: 508-872-0066/fax: 508-872-0020.

Dr. Charles Martin. Phone: 804-320-6800/fax: 804-320-1014.

FINANCIAL ADVISORS

Dennis Tubbergen. Phone: 231-924-6530/fax: 231-924-6836.

Michael Walters. Phone: 800-530-9872/fax: 800-280-5262.

MORTGAGE BROKERS

Reed Hoisington. Phone: 910-484-4519/fax: 910-485-3524.

Tracy Tolleson. Contact: www.tracytolleson.com.

REAL ESTATE AGENTS

Craig Proctor. Phone: 905-853-6135/fax: 905-853-6078 or visit Web site: www.craigproctor.com.

Craig Forte, Service for Life. Phone: 520-546-1349/fax: 520-546-1359.

REAL ESTATE INVESTORS

Ron LeGrand. Phone: 904-262-0491/fax: 904-262-1464 or visit Web site: www.GlobalPublishingInc.com.

RESTAURANTS

Rory Fatt. Phone: 604-940-6900/fax: 604-940-6902.

Michael Attias. Phone: 615-831-1676/fax: 615-831-1389.

RETAILERS

Bill Glazer. Phone: 800-545-0414 or www.bgsmarketing.com (Note: Bill is also publisher of Dan Kennedy's *No B.S. Marketing Letter,* information at www.dankennedy.com.)

Other Books by the Author

No B.S. Business Success, Entrepreneur Press

No B.S. Time Management, Entrepreneur Press

Ultimate Sales Letter, Adams Media

Ultimate Marketing Plan, Adams Media

Make Millions With Your Ideas, Penguin

The New Psycho-Cybernetics, Prentice-Hall

Zero Resistance Selling, Prentice-Hall

Author's Web Sites

www.dankennedy.com

www.dankennedyproducts.com

www.renegademillionaire.com

www.psycho-cybernetics.com

To Contact the Author Directly

Phone: 602-997-7707

Fax: 602-269-3113

Eternal Truths

Dan Kennedy's #1 No B.S. Truth About Selling

If you're going to achieve high levels of success in selling, you've got to be able to get positive results under negative circumstances.

•   •   •   •   •

Dan Kennedy's #2 No B.S. Truth About Selling

You don't have to be a psychic to read someone's mind—he or she will read it out loud to you, with a little encouragement!

•   •   •   •   •

Dan Kennedy's #3 No B.S. Truth About Selling

It's a good idea to learn from other people's experience but usually with this caveat: seek out and learn from those with experience who are at the top of their game.

•   •   •   •   •

Dan Kennedy's #4 No B.S. Truth About Selling

The logic is simple: if the packaging of products has an impact on how people regard those products, then the packaging of people must have an impact on how others regard those people.

•   •   •   •   •

Dan Kennedy's #5 No B.S. Truth About Selling

A top performer in selling is always focused on selling. A successful person takes this attitude, described by Zig Ziglar: you've got my money in your pocket, and I've got your product in my briefcase, and I ain't leaving until we make the exchange.

• • • • •

Dan Kennedy's #6 No B.S. Truth About Selling

Super-successful salespeople expect successful results.

• • • • •

Dan Kennedy's #7 No B.S. Truth About Selling

What others say about you and your product, service, or business is at least 1,000 times more convincing than what you say, even if you are 2,000 times more eloquent.

• • • • •

Dan Kennedy's #8 No B.S. Truth About Selling

In persuading others to part with their money, your best possible approach is demonstrating that the apparent expense is not an actual expense at all; that the thing being purchased is either free or, better yet, actually pays.

• • • • •

Dan Kennedy's #9 No B.S. Truth About Selling

If you're going to arrive at the sales presentation that achieves the maximum possible results, you're going to have to test a lot of different things that flop along the way.

• • • • •

Dan Kennedy's #10 No B.S. Truth About Selling

Your financial success will be very closely related to your ability to minimize your time spent meeting with people not qualified and ready to buy, and to maximize your time spent face-to-face with people who are qualified and ready to buy.

• • • • •

Dan Kennedy's #11 No B.S. Truth About Selling

Prospecting sucks.

• • • • •

Dan Kennedy's #12 No B.S. Truth About Selling

When have you ever heard of anybody going to see the wise man at the BOTTOM of the mountain?

Preface to

No B.S. Business Success

Just a spoonful of sugar helps the medicine go down.

—R. SHERMAN, FROM *MARY POPPINS*

Welcome to what I sincerely hope is the most truthful, blunt, straightforward, non-sugarcoated, no pabulum, no holds barred, no-nonsense, no B.S. book you have ever read on succeeding as an entrepreneur.

I wrote the first edition of this book back in 1993, and since then, I've personally heard from thousands of readers from all over the world. You saw a few of their comments on the opening pages of this book. It struck a chord with entrepreneurs; the chord of authenticity. No college classroom theory, no baloney. Real world truths from somebody who succeeds day in, day out, as an entrepreneur, working without a net. Since then, a lot has happened in my life, business and personal. For example, I've sold two businesses I built up; walked away from a very important and lucrative nine-year business relationship; made well-planned, continual, evolutionary changes in my other businesses; gone through a divorce after 22 years of marriage; been diagnosed diabetic; and more. I'm pleased to report I'm happier than I've been in many years and am living the life I set out to live.

Anyway, all these changes, new experiences, and lessons I've learned from my clients certainly warranted a complete updating of this book.

It is a personal book, me talking straight with you, as if I was consulting with you and as if we were sitting around at the end of the day on my deck, watching the sunset, enjoying adult beverages, and just hanging out. Because it is personal, along the way I'll be telling you quite a bit about me and about my business life—past, present, and future. None of this is about bragging. I have no need for that or interest in doing it. What I share, I tell you so that you understand the basis for the advice and opinions I dispense.

I have occasionally been introduced as The Professor of Harsh Reality. This does NOT mean I'm negative. If anything, I'm one of the most optimistic, positive-minded people you'll ever meet. However, I do not believe in confusing positive thinking with fantasy. And the word *optimism*, like many words in our perplexing English language, has more than one meaning. There's a mammoth difference between earned, deserved, justified optimism and wild-eyed, blue-sky, stubborn optimism.

I've discovered that I'm most successful when I have a firm grip on what is and least successful when caught wrestling with what ought to be.

In this book, I've tried to share, from my 25-plus years of entrepreneurial adventure, what *is*. Not what *should be* or what is only in theoretical books, classrooms, or seminar rooms.

If You Are Already in Business for Yourself

This book will help you go forward more astutely, efficiently, productively, and confidently. I think you'll also catch yourself nodding as you go along, saying to yourself, "This guy has been where I live." Sometimes there is value in just finding out you're not alone! The very first "success education" that I was ever exposed to was a set of recordings by Earl Nightingale titled *Lead the Field*, that I listened to when I was in my early teens. In those tapes, Nightingale gave me badly needed permission to violate the norms I saw around me, with his dramatic statement:

> *If you have no successful example to follow in whatever endeavor you choose, you may simply look at what everyone else around you is doing and do the opposite, because—THE MAJORITY IS ALWAYS WRONG.*

That may not be a precise, verbatim quote; but it is what I recall and have stored in my subconscious as a primary guiding principle. This leads to my strategy of deliberately questioning all industry norms, deliberately violating most of them, and encouraging my clients to do the same. It also led to my coining of the term "Mediocre Majority" to succinctly describe the vast undistinguished middle of any industry or profession. Anyway, Earl said a lot of things I had been thinking but had never heard anyone validate, and that gave me a great boost of confidence and conviction. Maybe some of my words, here, will do the same for you.

Most entrepreneurs tell me that the feeling they get from this book make them instantly eager to share it with other entrepreneurs. Please do so! If you want some place to send them, refer to www.nobsbooks.com.

If You Have Not Yet Started in Business but Intend To
This book might scare you off. If it does, consider it a favor; you're too easily spooked to succeed anyway. The entrepreneurial arena

is no place for the timid, nervous, or easily worried to come and play.

If it doesn't scare you off, it will help you avoid many pitfalls and problems and help you cope with those that can't be avoided. It will not cover the basics. There are plenty of books out there on the basics, and we're not going to cover the same ground all over again. This is not a how-to-start-a-small-business book. This is a go-for-the-jugular success book.

As I said earlier, I am not a fuzzy-headed academic, pocket-protector-and-wingtip-shoes accountant, or other theorist, although plenty of these pretenders write business books. I'm also not a retired authority who runs a business in my memory. I've been on the firing line meeting a payroll, battling the bankers and bureaucrats, struggling to satisfy customers, and solving real business problems. Over years, I've arrived at a point where my own business is engineered to meet all my lifestyle preferences— for example, only one employee, in a distant office, not under-foot; no set hours; no unscheduled phone calls. But still, I deal with clients and vendors and real business life just like you do. I also work very hands-on with clients in a wide variety of busi-nesses, as well as being "the consultant to the consultants"—I advise more than 50 different leading marketing and business consultants, each exclusively serving a different business or pro-fessional niche, in direct, hands-on relationships with more than one million small business owners. I want you to know this because I think it makes this book more valuable to you.

I'll never forget taking over a company with 43 employees, never having managed more than two people in my life. I grabbed every management book I could get my paws on and sucked up all the experts' advice. Then, after a couple of months of getting my brains beat in every day by my employees, I started to look critically at the credentials of those "expert" authors. Most of them had never—I repeat, never—managed a workforce. These geniuses spewing out creative management, nonmanipulative management, Japanese management, open-door management, and everything-else management wouldn't have survived a week in the real world. I resent those authors to this day. And it's a shame that a lot of college kids get that management theory, that is, fantasy sold to them as reality. So, I chucked all their books, rolled up my sleeves, used my common sense, and started finding out what really works and what doesn't.

Ever since then, I look at every new business book with suspicion. Most won't pass muster because most can't pass the real-experience test. I was originally motivated to write this book largely because reading most of the other books written for and sold to entrepreneurs turned my stomach.

I also want you to know that there are a lot more things I haven't got a clue about than there are things I understand; in this book, I have not dealt with any of the many things I'm in the dark about. Everything in here is based on my own expensive experience. It may not be right. You may not agree with it. But at least you should know that I didn't swipe it out of somebody else's book, give it a jazzy new psychobabble name, and pass it off as a new miracle tonic.

It's about Getting Rich

I also know you can't eat philosophy. So, although there is a lot of my own philosophy in this book, its primary job is to show you how to make more money then you ever imagined possible, faster than you can believe possible. This is a book about getting rich. If that offends you, please put this book back on the shelf or take it back to the store and get a refund. Spend your money on milk and cookies instead. You'll be happier. In fact, I'd like to quickly clear up a big misconception about what being an entrepreneur and owning and building a business is all about. The purpose is *not* to employ people, *not* to do social good, *not* to pay taxes. A lot of liberals think those are the purposes of business. Nuts to them. The purpose of being an entrepreneur is to get really, really rich, and reward yourself for taking on all the risk and responsibility with exactly the kind of life and lifestyle you want. Facilitating that is the sole aim of this book.

Before getting into the "meat," on the next few pages, you'll find a brief description of my business activities past and present and my current business in the back of the book beginning on page 247. I think you'll benefit more from the book if you understand where I'm coming from; however, you can choose to skip these pages if you like and jump right to Chapter 1. Your choice.

I'd like to explain the *Mary Poppins* quote at the top of this Preface. *Mary Poppins* was one of the first movies I was taken to see in a theater as a child. I watched it just the other night on cable TV and enjoyed it thoroughly. If you've seen it, you can probably call up the scene of Julie Andrews and the children singing the "just a spoonful of sugar helps the medicine go down" song. It's a lovely thought. (Or as she would say, "loverly.") In real business life, however, the emotional need for spoonfuls of sugar is very dangerous. How well you can take medicine— deal with reality—has a great deal to do with how successful you are as an entrepreneur.

There's a legendary book by Napoleon Hill I hope you've read, titled *Think and Grow Rich*. In that book, he enumerates 17 success principles adhered to in common by the hundreds of history's greatest entrepreneurial achievers he studied, interviewed and worked with, such as Andrew Carnegie, Henry Ford, Thomas Edison, and so on. Of the 17 principles, the one everybody seems to like the least and ignore the most is "accurate thinking." I believe it to be the most important one. So this book, my book, is heavy on that principle. It is medicine without the accompaniment of sugar.

Finally, let me say that, when I graduated high school, my parents were flat broke. I started with no family money. I didn't step into a family business. No one handed me anything on a silver platter. At age 49, I am semi-retiring, a multimillionaire, free to live precisely as I choose, indulging my interest in horse racing. It was all made possible through the kind of thinking, attitudes, habits, and strategies I've laid out in this book. I have been blunt, forthright, and held nothing back.

With that said, I still hope you not only profit from this book, but enjoy reading it. And I welcome your comments, thoughts, or questions. You can communicate with me directly by fax, 602-269-3113.

—Dan S. Kennedy

Preface to

No B.S. Time Management for Entrepreneurs

It gets late early out here.

—YOGI BERRA

Wimps and Willie Lomans—beware! This book is not for the faint of heart, fawningly polite, or desperate to be liked.

Hopefully, you have picked up this book because you are an entrepreneur, your time is incredibly valuable to you, and you are constantly "running out of it."

If you know me, then you've also been motivated to get this book to find out how I manage to do all that I do. I have been asked so often, by, what seems like everybody who becomes familiar with my life, how the devil I fit it all in, that I sat down and wrote out the answer—this book. If you don't know me, then your curiosity about my methods may be further piqued by the description of my activities that follow this Preface. If you know me, skip that section.

As a very busy, sometimes frantic, time-pressured entrepreneur, awash in opportunity, too often surrounded by nitwits and slower-than-molasses-pouring-uphill folk, I understand your needs, desires, and frustrations. The multiple demands on an entrepreneur's time are *extraordinary*. So I am here to tell you that you need to take extraordinary measures to match those demands. Measures so radical and extreme that others may question your sanity. This is no ordinary time management book for the deskbound or the person doing just one job. This book is expressly for the wearer of many hats, the inventive, opportunistic entrepreneur who can't resist piling more and more responsibility onto his own shoulders, who has many more great ideas than time and resources to take advantage of them, who runs (not walks) through each day. I'm you, and this is our book.

As you have undoubtedly discovered, time is the most precious asset any entrepreneur possesses. Time to solve problems. Time to invent, create, think, and plan. Time to gather and assimilate information. Time to develop sales, marketing, management, and profit breakthroughs. Time to network. Probably not a day goes by that you don't shove something aside, sigh, and say to yourself: *"If I could only find an extra hour* to work on this, it'd make a huge difference in our business." Well, I'm going to give you that extra hour. But what we're about to do here together is much bigger than just eking out an extra hour here or there. We are going to drastically re-engineer your entire relationship with time.

I've had more than 25 plus years of high-pressure, high-wire-without-a-net entrepreneurial activity—starting, buying, developing, selling, succeeding in and failing in businesses, going broke, getting profoundly rich, and helping clients in hundreds of different fields. Here's what I've come to believe to be the single biggest "secret" of extraordinary personal, financial, and entrepreneurial success combined: the use or misuse (or abuse by others) of your time—the degree to which you achieve peak productivity—will determine your success. So this book is about everything that can be done to achieve peak personal productivity.

Just thinking about it is a big step in the right direction. Awareness helps a lot. There's a reason why you can't find a wall clock in a casino to save your life—those folks stealing your money do not want you to be aware of the passing of time. And that tells you something useful right there: you want to be very aware, all the time, of the passing of time. It is to your advantage to be very conscious of the passage and usage of minutes and hours. Put a good, big, easily visible, "nagging" clock in every work area. If you spend a lot of time on the phone, have and use a timer.

Beyond simple awareness, there are practical strategies, methods, procedures, and tools that the busiest, most pressured person can use to crowbar some breathing room into his schedule, to force others to cooperate with his exceptional needs, to squeeze just a bit more out of each day. In this book, I give you mine. You will undoubtedly be interested in some, disinterested in others, maybe even repulsed by a few. That's OK. Although it's generally a bad idea to hire an advice-giver and then choose only the advice you like, in this case, it IS a cafeteria, and you can pick and choose and still get value.

Now it is time to get to work.

—Dan S. Kennedy

Index

Special Free Gift #1 from the Author

FREE Tele-Seminar with Dan Kennedy
How Top Sales Professionals Use Kennedy Style Marketing to Make Maximum Money—with No Cold Prospecting, Ever

Depending on when you redeem this certificate, you may be invited to a "live" tele-seminar at a particular date and time, which includes a question/answer opportunity, or if none are scheduled within 90 days of your request, you will be given a Web site and passcode to listen and/or download the audio of a "live" recording of one of these tele-seminars. Sold separately, this is a $95.00 value.

You will also receive the FREE REPORT: *The Five Chief Frustrations of Sales Professionals and How To Eliminate Them*, derived from a transcript of a speech Dan Kennedy prepared and presented for a major corporation's national sales organization.

TO OBTAIN YOUR FREE TELE-SEMINAR INVITATION AND FREE REPORT: There is no need to damage your book by tearing out this coupon—a photocopy is satisfactory. Complete ALL the information required, then either fax this form to 410-727-0978 or mail to Glazer-Kennedy Inner Circle, 200 W. Baltimore St., Baltimore, MD 21201. Allow 2 to 3 weeks for delivery. (Providing information below constitutes permission for Glazer-Kennedy Inner Circle to contact you with information about its products and services.)

Name _____

Business name _____

Address _____ ❏ Business ❏ Home

City/state/zip or postal code _____

Phone _____ Fax _____

E-mail address _____

FREE

Test Drive Three-Months of Dan Kennedy's
"Elite" Gold Inner Circle Membership

Receive a steady stream of marketing and business building advice

Yes Dan, I want to take you up on your offer of a FREE Three-Month Gold Inner Circle Membership, which includes:

1. Three months of your *No B.S. Marketing Newsletter*
2. Three months of your Exclusive Audiocassette Interviews
3. Three months of your Marketing Gold Hotsheet
4. Special FREE Gold Member Call-In Times
5. Gold Member Restricted Access Web Site
6. Continually updated Million Dollar Resource Directory
7. Open fax line
8. At least a 30% discount to future Glazer-Kennedy events and seminars

There is a one time charge of $5.95 to cover postage for ALL three months of the FREE Gold Membership and you have no obligation to continue at the *lowest* Gold Member price of $39.97 per month ($49.97 outside North America). In fact, should you continue with membership, you can cancel at any time by calling Glazer-Kennedy Inner Circle at 410-951-0147 or faxing a cancellation note to 410-727-0978.

Name _____ Business name _____

Address _____ ❑ Business ❑ Home

City/state/zip_____ E-mail _____

Phone _____ Fax _____

Credit card ❑ Visa ❑ MasterCard ❑ American Express

Credit card number _____ Exp date _____

Signature_____ Date _____

Providing this information constitutes your permission for Glazer-Kennedy Inner Circle LLC to contact you regarding related information via mail, e-mail, fax, and phone.